GREENWAR

ENVIRONMENT AND CONFLICT

by

Nafissa Abdel Rahim
Tafesse Hailu
Bernadette Ouédraogo
Babacar Touré
Mahamat Hissène
Berhane Woldegabriel
Zeremariam Fre
Nhial Bol Aken
Boubakar Ba
Omar Mohammed
Cheik Kolla Maïga

Edited by Olivia Bennett

THE PANOS INSTITUTE
Budapest - London - Paris - Washington

Published by Panos Publications Ltd
9 White Lion Street
London N1 9PD, UK

British Library Cataloguing in Publication Data
Greenwar: Environment and Conflict
1. West Africa
I. Rahim, Nafissa Abdel II. Panos Institute
333.70966
ISBN 1- 870670 - 23 - X

Greenwar is part of the Panos Sahel Programme, supported by the Danish International Development Agency (DANIDA), the Ford Foundation, the Netherlands Ministry of Foreign Affairs, the Norwegian Agency for Development Cooperation (NORAD), Oxfam (UK), and the Swedish Red Cross. Specific funding for *Greenwar* was provided by the Swedish Red Cross, Save the Children Fund (UK), Oxfam (UK), Oxfam (Canada), Christian Aid, and the Unitarian Universalist Committee.

Any judgements expressed in this document should not be taken to represent the views of any funding agency. Signed articles do not necessarily reflect the views of Panos or any of its funding agencies.

The Panos Institute is an information and policy studies institute, dedicated to working in partnership with others towards greater public understanding of sustainable development. Panos has offices in Budapest, London, Paris and Washington DC.

For more information about Panos contact:
Juliet Heller, The Panos Institute

Production: Sally O'Leary
Picture research: Adrian Evans
Cover design: Viridian
Maps: Philip Davies
Printed in Great Britain by The Lavenham Press Ltd, Sudbury, Suffolk

Contents

All indented quotes in bold have been taken from *At the Desert's Edge: Oral histories from the Sahel*, edited by Nigel Cross and Rhiannon Barker, Panos Publications, London, 1991

All currency conversions have been done at the February 1991 rate

INTRODUCTION
What is Greenwar?

For decades now, civil war has raged across Sudan, Ethiopia and Somalia. Violence has flared up more recently in Mauritania and Senegal, in Chad, in Mali and in Niger. Throughout the Sahel, tensions are increasing.

In some areas, periodic droughts have pushed a fragile environment to its limits, and famine has been the result. Centuries-old forms of land use are under growing pressure, forcing people to abandon their way of living. Uncounted thousands of Sahelians, displaced by drought, conflict or loss of traditional lands, are swelling refugee camps and shanty towns throughout the region.

It takes the overthrow of a government, as in Chad in 1990 and Somalia in 1991, or large-scale famine as in Sudan and Ethiopia in 1991 to bring events in the Sahel to international attention. This attention is often superficial, which serves to reinforce an image of the Sahel as permanently riven by strife and racked by hunger. The root causes of this tapestry of violence are poorly understood.

One key factor has been consistently neglected by politicians, diplomats, journalists and the military, within the Sahel as well as elsewhere. In the complex web of causes leading to social and political instability, bloodshed and war, environmental degradation is playing an increasingly important role. This is the Greenwar factor.

Throughout the Sahel, natural resources are diminishing. Competition over their use is increasingly tense, and violent conflicts—from a scuffle at a village well to tank battles in the Horn—are becoming more and more frequent. Governments are failing to concentrate on the conservation and equitable allocation of the resource base as a means of defusing conflict; instead, they

Ron Giling/Panos Pictures

A dried-up river bed in Mali. Drought is just one factor accelerating environmental decline and increasing conflict in the Sahel.

increasingly attempt to suppress conflict with short-term solutions. Sometimes this involves military activity, and many Sahelian governments are directing a large proportion of their expenditure into weaponry.

Massive military expenditure can suppress but never resolve underlying tensions. Peacekeeping which relies on military muscle, and ignores the Greenwar factor, is bound to be short-term.

The issues are complex and are the subject of an increasing amount of documentation and academic research. Development agencies and peace research organisations have attempted, during the 1980s, to explore more fully the causal links between environmental deterioration and political and military instability. In 1988 there was an international conference on Environmental Stress and Security, convened by the Royal Swedish Academy of Sciences. The United Nations Environment Programme (UNEP) has a programme on Peace, Security and the Environment, and UNEP has also been collaborating with the International Peace Research Institute (PRIO) in Oslo in looking at the issue of environmental security [1].

This book explores the issue from a different angle. *Greenwar* has been written by 11 Sahelian writers, who present a complex tapestry of case studies and interviews, interwoven with proverbs and legends. They draw on the first-hand experience of peasants and bandits, refugees and pastoralists, trying to unravel the tangled relationship between environmental decline, conflict and violence.

Their views are personal. These are not the analyses of outside experts, but the voices and opinions of women and men whose countries and lives are directly affected by the deteriorating situation in the Sahel. *Greenwar* tries to move beyond theoretical concepts and to present the perspectives and experiences of people for whom accelerating environmental decline and increasing conflict have been a reality. Their analyses of the links between the two phenomena demonstrate the complexities and the convictions involved. *Greenwar* is not written by dry academics. It tries to reflect some of the fears and hopes, the resignation and despair, the prejudices and the wisdom of the peoples of the Sahel. These voices must be heard if the issues are to be understood, let alone resolved.

Greenwar: the book

The authors do not argue that environmental degradation is ever the sole cause of conflict in the Sahel, or even always a major cause. But they do insist that the environment is an increasingly important factor, and that if the implications of ecological decline are not recognised, the prospects for the Sahel's future stability are bleak.

Competition for resources is not new. *Greenwar*'s first chapter puts the deteriorating situation in the Sahel in perspective, outlining the region's physical characteristics and some common environmental problems. It looks at traditional methods of land use, and at the reasons why some of these are now breaking down. Mauritanian Boubakar Ba offers an historical overview of the relationship of the Sahelian peoples with their environment. With the emergence of the modern state and its centralised and wide-ranging powers, local methods for controlling the use of farmland and pasture have been eroded. Pastoralists in particular have had little influence over government policies, and the agricultural sector has been forced into second place, after industrial development.

Chapter Two looks in more detail at the traditional competition for resources which has always been a feature of life in the Sahel. Cheik Kolla Maïga from Burkina Faso describes how different groups have developed powerful attachments to the resources around which their way of life has been built: grazing lands, ancient routes between dry- and wet-season pasture, or individual water sources. Chadian Mahamat Hissène describes how competition is so much part of the way of life in the Sahel that it is embedded in the culture of certain peoples.

As pressure on these natural resources increases, the balance between acceptable and unacceptable competition is more easily upset. Tension flares up into open hostility. Omar Mohammed writes about the complex series of kinship groupings in Somalia, which used to regulate the perpetual search by different clans for water and pasture in an arid land. The constantly shifting pattern of alliances and rivalries over grazing rights can break out into violent conflict, which in the 1950s led to serious intertribal war.

Ancient disputes

> **For herdsmen like us, our primary aim is to find good pasture...if we see a good field, full of crops, as long as we can use it to satisfy our animals, we do not mind paying for the damage after. Often these disputes turn into veritable wars, sometimes on such a grand scale that there are between 10 and 20 victims. It is like a war between two huge families; cultivators and pastoralists always support their own groups.**
> *Kaka Bouchia, pastoralist, Niger*

Chapter Three looks at the most fundamental area of rivalry and alliance in the Sahel, that between farmers and pastoralists. At its best, the relationship is a symbiotic one. Cattle graze the stubble of farmland, leave their manure and move on when the farmer needs to sow the soil. Mahamat Hissène writes about the Boulala people around Chad's Lake Fitri, who once had a close, mutually beneficial relationship with Arab nomadic herders who travelled to the lake in the dry season.

But such relationships can collapse under pressure. Unravelling the factors behind such breakdowns is a major concern of *Greenwar*. Babacar Touré gives his view of the way government policies in Senegal have increasingly marginalised the pastoralists and favoured those pursuing large-scale cultivation. He examines the prejudices held by both farming and nomadic groups as well as by policymakers, which he concludes have created a bitterness which will be hard to dispel. Eritrean Berhane Woldegabriel adds a detailed description of another group of pastoralists under threat: the Lahawin people in east Sudan. They face mounting pressures from the spread of government-supported mechanised farming. The Lahawin's access to resources is also threatened by the influx of refugees from Eritrea and by the robbers and bandits operating in the area, which has become increasingly violent and unstable.

The role of government

> **I think the government should recognise the hardship caused to the peasants when animals destroy their land. They should impose stricter sanctions against the badly behaved pastoralists, so that we may all begin to treat each other with more respect.**
> *Mbare Ndiaye, farmer, Senegal*

> **I think the government should be trying to tackle one regrettable problem, the issue of land reserved for pastoralists and farmers. At the moment, there are endless arguments between the two groups and I believe the government should be courageous and put strict limits on the amount of land to which each group is entitled.**
> *Abdoulaye Djibrilou, pastoralist turned farmer, Burkina Faso*

What role should the state play in such disputes over land and water? Despite the comparative weakness of much Sahelian government, the state has a major impact on people's lives. In exploring the Greenwar factor, almost all the authors found themselves examining the state's support for certain types of agriculture, its neglect and marginalisation of particular areas or groups, its failure to recognise and deal with potential environmental disaster and sometimes its direct encouragement of violence.

Nhial Bol Aken's contribution to Chapter Four looks at the conflict between Arabs and Fur in western Sudan, where he believes that government support for Arabs may be perpetuating the violence. The chapter also explores the situation of the Tuareg in Mali, whose resentment of official neglect and of their lack of political voice eventually erupted during 1990 into violent protest. Omar Mohammed gives his view of the reasons behind the civil war in Somalia, where increasing competition for resources was an important element in a complex web of causes.

Yet tensions can be defused before they escalate into violence, if governments act to protect and fairly share out the resource base. The four states bordering Lake Chad have succeeded in agreeing peaceful solutions to a potentially explosive situation, as more and more people are drawn to the lake's rich, but diminishing, resources.

The role of government is also a theme in Chapter Five, which explores conflicts over three transnational rivers: the Senegal, the Beli and the Nile. In the arid lands of the Sahel, competition for water has always been a central preoccupation. Rivers running through several states obviously have the potential to inspire clashes between as well as within countries. This chapter illustrates an important point in the Greenwar argument: the inadequacies of the concept of the independent nation state when it comes to natural resources. In the Sahel, ecological interdependence is indisputable and no state can ever resolve questions of resource use and allocation in isolation. Mechanisms to find workable solutions are needed throughout the Sahel, and other regions of the world .

The vicious circle

> Since my youth I have lived under the threat and insecurity of fighting. The first problems I remember were tribal...it must have been a dispute over rights either for water or for land. These are the only things that neighbouring tribes argue about.
> *Nizela Idriss, pastoralist, Chad*

> The relationship between different groups of pastoralists is not always amicable and may erupt when resources are low—particularly over the use of water in wells. Sometimes arguments...escalate into bloody battles where guns are used.
> *Hadi Ould Saleck, pastoralist turned farmer, Mauritania*

Another element in the Greenwar concept is that instability, precipitated by environmental pressures, in turn breeds further insecurity and violence. As traditional patterns of life break down, people often are forced into greater competition and conflict. In Chapter Six, Berhane Woldegabriel describes how dispossessed and economically marginalised pastoralists have become bandits, roaming the Sudanese-Ethiopian border and raiding farmers and nomads. Today, the easy availability of arms has raised the level of such violence. Babacar Touré describes how in Senegal many peasants have given up the struggle to farm, and have resorted to smuggling as a means of livelihood. Again, the use of firearms is escalating and the violence is spilling over into the wider community, as certain lands become "no-go" areas where law enforcement has all but broken down.

Full circle

Another kind of social breakdown is suffered by people who have been forced to give up their traditional livelihoods, because of drought, eroded or exhausted land or conflict. They have to move to shanty towns, to camps for the displaced or to new settlements, where their presence can cause more tension and conflict, as they compete with the local population for work and resources, and put further pressure on the surrounding environment. So the vicious circle continues. Chapter Seven looks first at the social and economic difficulties suffered by displaced women in Sudan and then at the Ethiopian government's resettlement policy.

Whole generations are growing up in the atmosphere of

instability and violence described in Chapters Six and Seven. The long-term effects are only just beginning to be felt, but are certain to increase the problems of the countries concerned.

The cycle is repetitive and truly vicious. Environmental impoverishment, increasing conflict over resources, marginalisation of rural people, social and political unrest, displacement and uncontrolled migration lead to further conflict and the outbreak of wars within and between states. When hostilities grow into organised warfare, the environment inevitably undergoes further degradation. The insidious pattern comes full circle, as a peacetime population and government struggle to cope with a land left environmentally bankrupt. The seeds are sown for further tension and conflict. In Chapter Eight, Zeremariam Fre describes in detail the impact of decades of war on Eritrea, and the problems this will pose for future generations.

Responses

Greenwar ends with some preliminary conclusions. Nobody will agree with everything, and some organisations or governments may disagree violently with parts of the text. *Greenwar* does not set out to be comprehensive and its grassroots emphasis has necessitated selectivity and the inclusion of much anecdotal material. But the Sahelian authors present important perspectives, draw attention to little-considered aspects of social upheaval, and demonstrate convincingly that environmental degradation, in the Sahel at least, is an increasingly significant element in conflict.

Today, when profound political changes are being discussed in countries right across the Sahel, the Panos Institute hopes that this book will contribute to a debate which must pay far greater attention to the implications of environmental decline.

The researching and writing of *Greenwar* has been a collaborative venture. But it presents a far from complete picture. Rather, it offers a close look at a mere handful of the thousands of stories which make up the complex mosaic of Sahelian reality. Panos alone has been responsible for the selection and editing of each contribution. In particular, no individual author can be held responsible for the overall balance or the conclusions of this book.

Nigel Twose
The Panos Institute

CHAPTER ONE

The Sahel
Climate, land use and social structure

Sahel is an Arabic word meaning border or shore. The Sahel is precisely that: a border of marginal land, 500-1,000 km wide, separating the Sahara desert from the tropics further south. It stretches 7,000 km from west to east, from the Atlantic beaches of Senegal across to the Red Sea, running along the southern edge of the Sahara until broken up by the hills and mountains of Ethiopia and Somalia.

In 1973, the largely francophone states in the western part of the region used the term Sahel to define the organisation which they had established for collective action against drought: the Inter-State Committee for Drought Control in the Sahel (CILSS). This effectively cut the ecological zone in half, stopping at the linguistic border between Chad and Sudan. The equivalent body for the eastern Sahel, the Inter-Governmental Authority on Drought and Desertification (IGADD), whose member countries are Uganda, Somalia, Kenya, Djibouti, Ethiopia and Sudan, was established in the mid-1980s. This book explores the relationship between environmental degradation and conflict in nine countries which stretch right across the Sahel: in Senegal, Mauritania, Mali, Niger, Burkina Faso, Chad, Sudan and Somalia as well as in Ethiopia, including the disputed territory of Eritrea.

Early history

Between 5500 BC and 2500 BC the Sahara was well-watered savanna. Throughout this period, the region's forests, rivers and grassland plains flourished. People in the swamps and marshes of

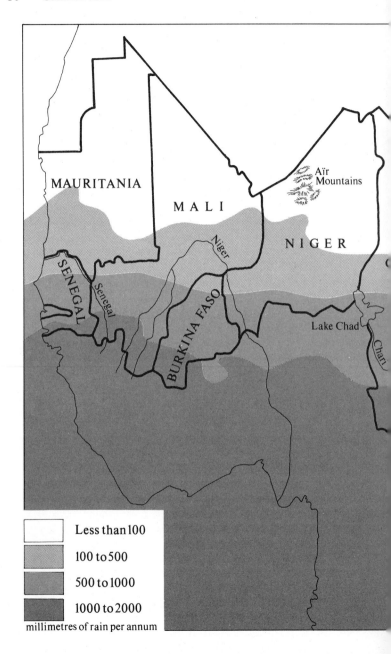

Less than 100

100 to 500

500 to 1000

1000 to 2000

millimetres of rain per annum

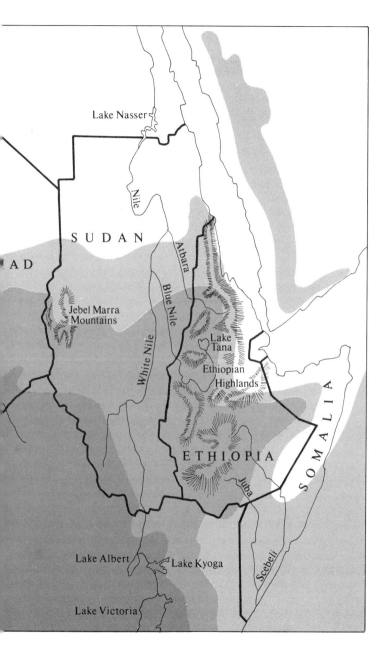

the Nile valley had already learned to grow food by regular tilling and irrigation. The Saharans, too, began agricultural production around 3500 BC, while grazing their great herds of horned cattle on the rich pastureland. The Saharan-Sudanese community was the first in Africa to practise farming on any significant scale [1].

From about 2000 BC, the Sahara has been slowly drying out. Some of the rivers which made up the region's massive water system have disappeared; others now only run after the rains.

The region today

The Sahara today is desert and in the semi-arid lands of the Sahel rainfall is limited and variable, ranging between 150 mm and 600 mm a year. The rains usually come in a four-month period, falling largely in July and August. This gives most farmers, outside the irrigated areas, one main annual harvest and herders three months of good pasture.

Taken together, the nine countries of the Sahel have a current population of around 120 million. Some 75% of Sahelians depend on livestock and agriculture for their living. Agriculture is restricted by the low rainfall but, even so, the Sahelian belt is characterised today by a consistent expansion of cultivated land. In Senegal, for instance, farmers increased the amount of land under cultivation by 8,000 sq km (an area just under the size of Cyprus) during the 20 years up to 1986. In Ethiopia, an additional 20,000 sq km were put under cultivation during the same 20-year period [2]. The few mountain chains in the region, where rainfall is higher and which have been cultivated intensively for centuries, are suffering from severe soil erosion and a rapid depletion of forest and bush cover. Pressures on the cultivated lowlands are consequently growing in severity.

Such generalisations mask wide disparities in a geographically diverse region. The Ethiopian highlands, for example, home of the ancient civilisation of Axum, rise up in places to over 3,000 metres, and are sliced across by the Rift Valley and surrounded by lowlands. Plough cultivation is generally practised in the highlands, while the lowlands support both sedentary farming and nomadic pastoralism. Neighbouring Somalia remains predominantly pastoral. There is great variation within areas, too, since rainfall is highly localised and unpredictable. Nonetheless, there is enough ecological cohesion across the Sahel to justify looking at it as one region.

Ron Giling/Panos Pictures

"When the land is no longer fruitful and the authorities have abandoned us...". Drought and land degradation have forced some farmers to resort to smuggling, banditry or migration to survive.

Drought

One common feature is the recurrence of drought. In this century alone, there have been periods of drought between 1910 and 1914, around 1930 and from 1940 to 1944. Prolonged and extensive drought returned to the Sahel in 1968 and an international disaster was declared in 1973 when the rains failed for the sixth consecutive year. In Sudan, some referred to that drought as *ifza 'una* ("rescue us"). In 1984, Sudan was undergoing the worst drought this century, and the later droughts in Sudan and Ethiopia which began at the end of the 1980s may prove to be equally severe.

Understanding and predictions of global warming are still uncertain. But there is no doubt that the precarious nature of the Sahelian environment means "that the people of the Sahel suffer disproportionately from changes in global weather. Rainfall in the Sahel depends upon the reach of the Inter-Tropical Convergence Zone (ITCZ), the equatorial rendezvous for tropical air masses. In the summer months, warm maritime air condenses into monsoon clouds; how far north the clouds reach depends on the relative strength of atmospheric circulations over the oceans, which in turn may be affected by small differences in sea temperatures between the North and the South Atlantic. If the ITCZ contracts a fraction, the consequence for Sahelian farmers at the edge of the rainfall belt is certain crop failure [3]."

Nobody knows how many people died in the drought of the early 1970s; there is no agreement on whether the figure was thousands or hundreds of thousands. But it is clear that the effects of drought in the Sahel are not socially uniform. Drought magnifies existing social and economic inequalities, which are already exacerbated by ecological disruption.

Degradation—an escalating problem

"Degradation" is defined as a fall in biological productivity. Such a definition is a relative one, since measurement is according to human expectations and is dependent on the technologies practised. It is not a recent phenomenon. Six thousand years ago, poor irrigation practices in Mesopotamia and Babylon caused huge tracts of land to become salinised and food production to collapse [4].

Throughout the Sahel, degradation often, though not exclusively, takes the form of "desertification". Desert conditions appear where they did not previously exist, and the soil yields progressively less. The popular image of the desert taking over farmland at the rate of several kilometres a year is inaccurate. The spread of the desert is more like a bad skin disease. It appears wherever people or governments have exhausted land by overexploiting its potential; individual patches then join together, until eventually a whole area is affected. Typically, the underground water table falls, the soil dries out and its humus content and fertility drop, vegetation dwindles and wildlife begins to disappear.

Today there is another, more sinister form of degradation in the war-torn regions of the Sahel: areas of land have been defoliated, burned or polluted with chemicals, or can no longer be managed productively because of landmines. But there are also conflict areas where the reverse has happened: abandoned land has become restocked with vegetation and wildlife because humans and livestock no longer overexploit it.

Typically, degradation and its social costs affect at first only the rural poor. Increasing numbers of people live in environmentally fragile areas with little potential for improving their situation. Poverty fuels further deterioration, driving desperate people to overexploit their resource base, sacrificing the future to salvage the

Ron Giling/Panos Pictures

"It is for lack of other produce that I sell wood, because at least I am sure that it will be bought and that I will have enough money to provide for my needs."

present. **Bernadette Ouédraogo**, director of a women's non-governmental organisation (NGO) in Burkina Faso, relates a conversation she had with Rasmata, a village woman, carrying a huge load of firewood.

"Why do you travel such a long distance with this load of wood and your baby on your back?"

"What a question! My baby is ill. I nursed her with traditional medicine but the illness persisted. My husband and I decided that I would take her to the clinic in Ouagadougou—there is no clinic in our village—and as we don't have any cash, I brought some wood which I am going to sell. With the takings from the wood, I will be able to buy the modern medicine the nurse will prescribe."

"Don't you know that it is the excessive cutting of trees that is causing the advance of the desert into our country?"

"What can we do? When I was a girl, there were many fruits to be gathered. We kept a third for our own consumption, and sold the remainder in town; we would simply take the fruits and leaves without jeopardising the life of the tree. Now these trees are rare and you have to go a long way to find them.

"We used to collect firewood from trees which had died naturally. Now there aren't any. We have to go a long way, to cut living shrub and leave it to dry out for days or weeks before we can use it for our fires. It is for lack of other produce that I sell wood, because at least I am sure that it will be bought and that I will have enough money to provide for my needs."

As degraded ecosystems offer diminishing yields to their poor inhabitants, a downward spiral of economic deprivation and environmental degradation takes hold. The poor are forced into competing for resources they used to share, and conflict all too often

Bernadette Ouédraogo

Burkinabè women work together to avoid conflict over a shared but diminishing water source.

results. Bernadette Ouédraogo talked to the head of a village women's group in Burkina Faso who related the story of one such conflict, which in this case was resolved peacefully.

"In our grandparents' time there was an abundance here, and people from different villages tried to outdo each other in kindness. Today it is different, because there isn't enough rain, the harvests are bad and the men are less kind. These problems cause all sorts of conflicts. One no longer hesitates to shoot down a neighbour's goat that is found in one's field.

"Badnogho II and Tanlarghin are two neighbouring villages which were friendly for a long time. But since the 1980s the good relationship of the past has disappeared. Why so? Because of environmental degradation.

"Consecutive droughts caused such a shortage of drinking water that the women of the two villages started quarrelling over the well.

"Some of them began to wonder which of the two villages this well, dug decades ago, belongs to. They wanted to insist that the owners have priority over its use. What a disaster! People became tense, exchanging unfriendly remarks. Fortunately for both sides, people realised what was happening and the two villages were reconciled. Something good has come out of misfortune, for now we work together to look for answers to our problems. But it could have ended in tears!"

Pastoralism

> **The growing number of farmers in the area threatens our existence....Agricultural land has been so drastically extended that all we can do is dream of the vast pastures which once stretched out before us. The pastures left to us have suffered from erosion from the wind and the rain.**
> *Peulh (Fulani) pastoralists, Niger*

Pastoralism—looking after herds of cattle, sheep, goats and camels—has been characteristic of the Sahel for centuries, especially on the northern fringes where rainfall is lowest. In the twentieth century, economists, politicians and planners have tended to dismiss the practice as primitive and inefficient. Pastoralism has been neglected or even deliberately suppressed, and nomads have been forced or urged to settle and take up agriculture or city life.

But nomadism, in which wandering herders track down pockets of good pasture, and transhumance, which involves the regular movement of livestock between established seasonal pastures, in fact make rational and skilled use of marginal land.*

Some recent research shows that the ecological efficiency of pastoralist economies can often be as great as, or greater than, the intensive farming of industrialised countries [5]. The animals convert sparse vegetation into milk and meat, and provide wool and hides; manure on farmers' fields is a valuable by-product. In particular, since rainfall in the Sahel is highly variable and localised, the flexibility of nomadism is the only real way to exploit a sudden growth of rich vegetation in a few hectares of land which may see no more rain for the next five or ten years. Transhumance, with its cycle of planned migration within traditionally defined areas, gives the vegetation periods of time when it is not grazed or trampled on by animals and so allows it to regenerate.

Today, this centuries-old balance between people and nature is under threat, right across the Sahel. Pastoralists are becoming poorer and poorer, and in many cases finding it impossible to survive.

Why is this happening? Drought obviously reduces, temporarily, the resources available to livestock. Drought can sometimes also lead indirectly to long-term or permanent degradation of the land, when pastoralists are forced to roam within smaller and smaller areas and thus to overgraze the vegetation, preventing regeneration, and to overexploit the water sources. But drought is not the only factor at work. The impoverishment of pastoralists and small farmers has been heavily influenced by official development patterns and priorities.

---

* Although nomadism and transhumance are distinct forms of land use with different social systems, they are often referred to together. In this book, as in many others, nomadism is often used to include transhumance.

Changing patterns

Boubakar Ba, a Mauritanian socio-economist currently based in Senegal, looks at the changes which have taken place in Sahelian society, particularly in the western states, and how these have affected people's relationship with their environment. He argues that the sharing of resources became more and more complex as groups with increasingly differentiated and competing economic interests developed. The process reached a peak with the emergence of the modern state, with its centralised and wide-ranging powers.

Land management in the Sahel
by Boubakar Ba

As long as people have inhabited the Sahel, their main concern has been to manage their land and organise their economic activities rationally within the available habitable space. In the past, they respected the laws of nature and maintained the balance between people and environment. After cultivation they left land fallow for long periods to allow it to recover; their transhumant herding patterns allowed vegetation to be renewed every year; and they resorted to migration when natural disaster made life in a particular area impossible. The carrying capacity of an area was not exceeded; natural resources were not used up faster than they could replenish themselves.

In desert or semi-desert areas herding predominated, and agriculture was confined to the oases; in the more humid southern zones, agriculture was the key activity and herding was exceptional. Between the two zones was an intermediate area, where the two activities co-existed and sometimes conflicted, usually as a result of climatic conditions, especially changes in rainfall patterns.

As time went on the population increased, while the overall climatic conditions deteriorated. Traditional solutions proved to be inadequate to deal with the increasing pressures on the environment.

During the last 100 years, the Sahelian economy and society have undergone profound changes, moving from land management based on kinship/lineage relationships to a capitalistic agrarian economy, which has absorbed the slave labour and tenant farming systems which had grown up in earlier centuries, when the empires of

Ghana, Mossi, Songhai, Kanem-Bornu and others dominated the Sahel.

One characteristic of kinship/lineage relationships is the common management of land resources in the form of joint-tenancy arrangements. Land belonged to a patriarchal family or tribal clan, and was redistributed periodically amongst the members of that group. This land was inalienable: each adult male member was allocated a plot which he had the right to use but not to own. Today this practice has become the exception in the Sahel, although in certain groups it remains a convenient fallback, given the reduced size of landholdings, as it is among the Soninke of Mali, Mauritania and Senegal. The best lands are allocated to the *teexore* (collective field) of the patriarchal family, and only then are individual plots shared out. Most of the men's available time, especially at sowing and harvest, is given to work in the *teexore*.

Slave labour was organised on the basis that the slave worked the fields of his master, who fed and maintained him but who retained exclusive rights over the harvest and all land resources. Slaves subsequently became serfs, who still laboured most of the time in their lords' fields but who had rights to the produce from a plot of land allocated by their former owners for their use.

Agrarian practices based on serfdom continued to exist alongside the new labour relationships of modern irrigated agriculture: agrarian capitalists and agricultural labourers. Indeed, a particular characteristic of capitalism in the rural Sahel is the way that it has incorporated features of the old system.

The development of capitalist agriculture, and the new land-tenure legislation introduced by successive governments from colonisation until today, appreciably altered traditional means of distributing and managing land. As the struggle between old and new intensifies, great upheaval results, through which small-scale peasant producers, sometimes voluntarily cooperating in groups, seek with difficulty to chart a safe course.

People's participation

The different sectors of Sahelian economies—herding, agriculture, industry—have always competed for natural resources. Today they also compete for power within the state.

Herders are now at the bottom of the pile. The groups which control state power in the Sahelian countries which are members of

CILSS (Senegal, Mauritania, Niger, Mali, Burkina Faso, Chad, Cape Verde, The Gambia and Guinea Bissau) act as representatives of sedentary farmers rather than herders as far as agricultural policy is concerned. They almost always settle disputes in favour of their communities of origin, designing development projects which marginalise nomadic herders and formulating land management policies which neglect the specific interests of the pastoralists—thus disqualifying the state from being the arbitrator it should be. The two exceptions to this are Mauritania and Chad, where representatives of nomadic herder groups enjoy power in the state machinery.

Following their independence, the CILSS countries implemented economic policies which gave overall pride of place to industrial projects, and relegated agricultural development to second position. The new leaders increasingly represented the emerging urban classes and were more interested in maintaining stability in the towns. Even when harvests were satisfactory, the agricultural sector was unable to accumulate the necessary resources to ensure progress, due to the lack of any policy to support, protect and develop national production.

Moreover, even when projects did concern peasants, they neither developed from the concerns of these small farmers, nor made those concerns a priority. Governments decided for the peasants how best to ensure their wellbeing, and operated in an authoritarian way. In the rare cases where genuine efforts were made, the end result too often simply reproduced traditional hierarchies serving minority interests, and did nothing to educate and train the mass of the people.

These are the root causes of the destruction of the former framework which governed land use, and which coordinated collective efforts, however limited, to protect and improve the environment.

Democracy

In rural areas of the Sahel today, the demand for democracy is essentially linked to the urgent need to loosen the grip of centralised state control and to establish the conditions for local people to take charge of their own destiny—especially with regard to land management, and environmental protection and improvement.

The growing demands for democracy in Africa and other parts of the world might help in the Sahel to bring about decentralisation and to foster greater management by the people of their own resources. But this is by no means certain. Although current economic thinking emphasises free enterprise in the framework of so-called structural adjustment policies, it pays scant attention to small-scale peasant production, or to voluntary cooperation based on the past experience of the rural populations of the region.

CHAPTER TWO

Traditional Competition

In the arid and semi-arid lands of the Sahel, agricultural activity has never been easy. A drier year than usual, floods, or a sudden increase in the number of people using a particular piece of land or water source, can destroy the fine line between plenty and scarcity. People learned to live mostly on the right side of the line by moving around, diversifying their production, storing food from year to year and protecting their own resources.

Different groups have developed strong emotional and cultural ties to the water points and lands they have traditionally used. **Cheik Kolla Maïga**, a Burkinabè journalist who writes for the national newspaper *Sidwaya* in Ouagadougou, relates an incident from the Beli River area on the border between Mali and Burkina Faso. The story shows how strongly, and in some cases perhaps almost irrationally, people are attached to their heritage.

The taste of water
by Cheik Kolla Maïga

For a long time there has been no new development of water resources in the semi-desert Beli River area in Burkina Faso. The river and the surrounding pools are the only near-permanent water points in the entire area. Six boreholes exist in the department of Tin-Akoff, three of them in the town of Tin-Akoff. But whether because of the lack of pump maintenance at the boreholes or purely from custom, the great majority of the population remains deeply attached to the "natural" sources. Indeed, when questioned about their sources of water, people often omitted to point out the working wells; they use the river or the ponds instead, even though the wells are cleaner, because "it was always thus since our parents' times".

Everywhere we went, we were offered water to drink. This cloudy liquid came straight from the Beli River, and the people would tease us when they saw our reluctance to drink it. "Here we are immune," they would say mockingly. Even when the nearby well was in working order, they often preferred to drink this whitish water—which they believe is harmless, for them at least! In fact, most diseases in the area derive from it.

Yet the many cases of amoebiasis, guinea worm, kidney problems, dysentery and bilharzia do not seem to discourage them. This has particularly grave implications for children, and health workers constantly try to make parents aware that the consequences of their deep-seated attachment to the river water can be serious. In Tin-Akoff, we met a man of 60 or so who was rushed off to the infirmary because he had been unable to urinate for three days. A catheter was inserted, and we could see the mud oozing out of the device. In spite of his relief, and two further days of treatment which finally cleared the blockage in his urinary system, he confessed that he would not be able to give up drinking the Beli River water, because its taste was much nicer than that of the well in his village of Kacham. In reply to the suggestion that he should boil the water before drinking it, he smiled. "We haven't got much time for that, with our many wanderings!"

The culture of competition

Sometimes the pastoralists cause trouble on purpose just because they want to tease the farmers, whom they blame for the fact that much of their grazing land is no longer available.
Gawa Assoumane, farmer, Niger

Over the years, rights of access to land and water have undergone adjustments, so that different groups have customary areas they use and water sources they share with neighbouring groups. But every group, whether village, tribe or family, has to be vigilant to protect its rights against others driven by the same need. So competition has always been part of life in the Sahel and many cultures incorporate and celebrate it, as **Mahamat Hissène**, a journalist with the Ministry of Information in Chad, illustrates in this story.

Tensions and alliances
by Mahamat Hissène

Adoum's memories are similar to those of many herdsmen in Chad.
He mentions his fights without any resentment. Far up north, during
the rainy season, Adoum and his cousins met some camel herdboys
and they had a fight. Adoum was roughed up but the boys said
nothing to their parents. Then, at the end of the rainy season, on their
way south towards central Chad, they and their oxen were
challenged by some village children. The two groups shouted abuse
and threw lumps of mud at each other, until their oxen stopped
drinking and Adoum and his group went away with their herd.

At Lake Fitri, during the hot season, Adoum achieved a real feat
of war. Some farmers tried to keep one of his young bulls as
compensation for damage caused in their fields the night before.
The field owners blamed Adoum's herd, but he claimed that his
animals had nothing to do with it. The young boy struggled with
such force that the farmers finally released his animal.

"Once I had got away," he said, "just to annoy them, I shouted,
'It *was* my oxen yesterday, you horrible people!'"

The motive for this incident seems clear enough, but I asked
Adoum why the herdsmen fight among themselves. He replied, "It's
not serious. It's for play, and we don't use any sharp weapons."

Ritual provocation

As soon as they see another herd, the pastoralists try to identify its
keepers. If they are not relatives or close allies, the two groups weigh
each other up and those who feel stronger start the provocation
ritual.

"Hey you! Take your horrible fly-ridden cows away, and
quickly!"

"You move yours first!" comes the defiant answer, out of pride
or just because the others feel like some action.

Such encounters often follow rules, the goading beginning with
the youngest elements in the groups, sometimes girl against girl and
so on, two by two, until the eldest become involved. A general
scuffle then ensues.

When it is noticed within a group that a young girl or boy does
not relish these frays, the peer group unites and tries to force her or
him to conform. The family must never find out that their youngster

was scared of taking up a challenge. How shameful! Isn't this the way to prepare young people to face life?

In the areas criss-crossed by Adoum and his people, farmers and livestock herders share the use of huge tracts of land. Everyone must assert their authority to get access to water, pasture, wild fruit and berries. Everyone has virtually the same legal rights to the land and its resources, except in areas with specially dug wells and fields. Real fights are rare. And knowing how to avoid them is as important as winning them. Generally speaking, encounters never go much further than a simple challenge, but excesses are always possible.

Water: source of life and power

Seasonal movement remains an essential part of land management in Chad. Even more than land, a watering place is the prize possession, the one which endows a group with great authority, whether it has inherited a natural source, or created new wells.

Digging a traditional well takes titanic efforts. Men use rudimentary tools and bring soil to the surface in scoops, drawn by the donkeys, bulls or camels which will be used later to draw up the precious water. Plaited straw reinforced with branches forms the

Jeremy Hartley/Panos Pictures

In an arid land, the search for water is the preoccupation around which social and economic life revolves.

well-lining. Traditional wells need frequent repairs, which are carried out by all current users.

The owners of a well have eternal rights over it. They organise rotas for use during busy periods, and rationing. More rarely, they reserve a time of day or a side of the well where they alone can place their pulley. At such times, the men frequently fight over the rotas. The more timid have to wait longer.

Because of the power invested in a well, the head of each clan does all he can to prevent others from digging one on his territory. When the government (formerly colonial, now Chadian) digs wells in traditional nomad areas, each clan asserts its authority over those dug in its territory.

In some areas of Chad, water is not far below the surface; each family or caravan can dig a well, often in the dried-up bed of a seasonal river. In order to avoid overgrazing in those areas, herders forbid the building of two wells within a radius that would put two herds in the same pasture. In this way, the customary chiefs ensure a better livestock spread over a given area.

Southward bound

Nomadic herders who own large herds, especially of cattle, cannot remain long during the dry season in the pastures of the northern Sahel. Watering a whole herd of oxen at the well daily is an exhausting chore. Wells are deep, often as much as 60 metres, and the water level gets lower and lower as the dry months go on.

During the big heatwaves, families camp permanently beside the wells. The shriek of the wooden pulleys and the nervous calls of the teenagers who direct the draught animals echo day and night, mixed with the lowing of the thirsty animals. Tempers fray easily and if a rope is badly engaged or a clay watering trough is torn apart by an animal, the worst can happen. The tension is relentless.

Although a lot of camel herders in Chad put up with this work throughout the dry season until the rains come, most cattle herders are forced to move early on to the centre of the country, nearly 200 km away. This migration, and the return back north at the onset of the rains, are rich in symbolic value. Indeed, the words used to refer to these periods have almost replaced the names of the seasons in ordinary speech. Each group follows a fixed route and camps in the same areas every year. For the Batha Arabs, for instance, the main dry-season gathering point is Lake Fitri (see Chapter Three).

From competition to conflict

In a context of perpetual tension, the balance between acceptable and unacceptable rivalry can be easily upset, by drought or by other factors. **Omar Mohammed**, a Somali journalist, illustrates how fiercely certain groups identify with their traditional lands and resources. He explains how the complex alliances and rivalries built into Somalia's kinship system can erupt into war when dwindling resources force one clan to intrude upon another's territory.

Clan against clan
by Omar Mohammed

Somalis are one ethnic group with one language (Somali) and one religion (Islam): something rare for an African country. Strong ideological differences have not yet developed among groups. The destructive war Somalis have been waging against one another might seem incompatible with this apparent homogeneity, but it is proof that homogeneity alone does not ensure a peaceful and stable society, and that there are other factors which are as important, and which deserve equal attention.

The majority of Somalia's 8 million people are nomads, owning between them about 50 million animals. Pressure has always been intense on the available pasture and water. At best the climate is arid, with an average rainfall of 500 mm per year, mainly in spring and autumn. But failure of the rains has been characteristic of the Somali ecosystem, and during this century alone there have been 13 droughts, some of them catastrophic. Foremost among these was the devastating drought of 1926-29 which destroyed as much as 80% of the total sheep and goat population [1]. The Somali saying "Calamities are adaptable" indicates how common these disasters are, and how the people manage to survive them. "Abundance and scarcity are never far apart," goes another Somali saying. "The rich and the poor frequent the same houses."

During the dry season, people and herds concentrate around the limited number of wells. During the rainy season, the overgrazed land around the water points is abandoned, and the nomads' *aqal* (portable huts) are loaded onto the backs of *rarey* (burden camels) and the livestock moved to broader, richer pastures.

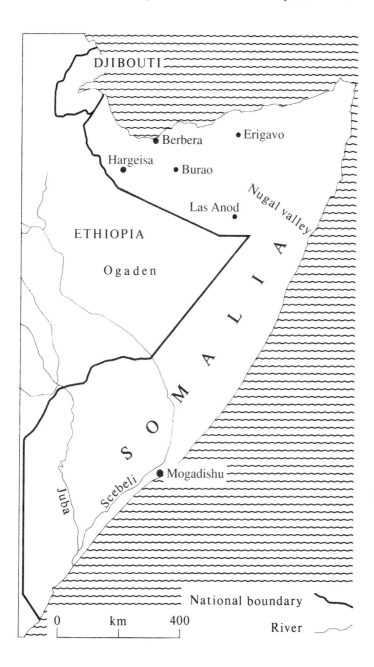

Berbera

Erigavo

Hargeisa

Burao

DJIBOUTI

Las Anod

Nugal valley

ETHIOPIA

Ogaden

SOMALIA

Mogadishu

Juba

Scebeli

National boundary

River

0   km   400

Good rains bring times of joy and plenty. Fresh green grass abounds and milk is plentiful. Animals bring forth their young, since the nomads regulate their breeding so that they reproduce after the spring or autumn rains when sufficient grazing can be expected. Everyone talks of peace and plenty. "Somali pastoralists equate war with drought, and oppose these conditions to those of peace and plenty....People who in the rigours of the dry season regime had become thin and weak recover their strength and vigour [2]." This seasonal physical change among the people is very noticeable, and parallels a similar variation in the condition of livestock.

The situation begins a gradual reverse twice a year, towards the end of each three-month rainy season. The green grass fades, warning of its eventual death. Livestock yield less and less milk until they stop. The levels in shallow wells and temporary lakes drop, and eventually they dry up; the deep wells reach a point where only a vertical human chain can bring up the water, tossing skin-buckets from man to man.

As the gradual withering of all the sources of life announces the return of the harsh dry season, the nomads cease their rainy-season "leisure" activities. Marriages and *haasaawe* (chatting with members of the opposite sex) rarely happen in the dry season, and are strongly advised against. Religious feasts stop and even the memory of God is put aside, along with His suspension of resources.

The movements of the Somali nomads and their herds are directed by the seasons and by the availability of water. However, there are some restrictions. The limited resource base makes every nomad a potential enemy in the eyes of the other, so competition and the need for security are regulated by a complex system of kinship groupings.

The Somali kinship system

Some knowledge of this kinship system is essential to understanding the migration, competition and conflict patterns of Somali nomads. With few exceptions, all Somalis belong to one of six kinship groupings, or clan-families. The four main clan-families—Dir, Isaaq, Hawiya and Daarood—are predominantly nomadic pastoralists, while the other two—Digil and Rahanweyn —are mainly agriculturalists. Despite their common physical features, language, religion and culture, these six groups do not believe that they are of common origin. Members of each group trace their descent from a single male ancestor, independent from the ancestors of the other clan-families. Intermarriage is widespread among the six groups, but maternal blood does not count as far as clan identity is concerned.

Each of the six clan-families is subdivided into smaller groups, or clans, whose average size is over 3,000. The clans in turn are subdivided, down through several levels of smaller and smaller groups, ending with the *jilib* or *dia* (blood-money) paying group. Of all the divisions, it is the second level, the clan, which is most important in terms of conflict.

These many layers of alliance reflect the different levels at which competition takes place and the need for security exists. Both alliance and rivalry are seen as equally necessary by the Somali nomad, even at the level of the nuclear family, as this Somali saying shows: "If you have a son, make sure you have a brother, and if you have a brother make sure you have a son."

Every person is a member of several alliances or subgroups. Different conditions determine the relative importance of these various identities, so a nomad's political allegiance is constantly shifting. The clan-family, as a group, is large and widely dispersed. Its size, and the marginal resources of the country, make the clan-family less an alliance than an association of rival and competing clans.

The clan has a regular pattern of seasonal movement, and a loosely defined traditional territory. Each clan territory contains wells, usually excavated by the clan's members, and pastureland. During the dry season, each clan moves to concentrate around its few wells. These are often in an overexploited part of the territory, and the water is insufficient. To reduce the likelihood of conflict, subgroups settle together in hamlets formed of close relatives.

There is an overlap in the orbits of different clans, which inevitably results in clashes over access to common resources. The area of overlap increases in times of drought, as one clan may intrude further into the territory of another when its own natural resources become too meagre. This cycle—the decline of resources forcing one clan to intrude upon another, leading to mutual hostilities—is something with which the Somali nation has always lived. One of the most disastrous wars of this kind was the 1951-57 Hargaga war between the Habarje'lo clan (of the Isaaq clan-family) and the Dhulbahanta clan (of the Daarood clan-family).

The Hargaga war

The Habarje'lo clan territory extends from the east to the west of northern Somalia and includes parts of the eastern Ogaden region in Ethiopia. The Dhulbahanta clan borders the Habarje'lo to the south almost throughout the length of its territory.

Some eastern subgroups of the Habarje'lo moved south of their border to the rich Nugal valley, which was at the time in Dhulbahanta territory. The Dhulbahanta elders asked the Habarje'lo to withdraw. The Habarje'lo elders claimed that they had certain rights in the disputed area since the clouds which rained there form first in their northern highlands. They also said that the valley was indispensable for their animals' survival. The Dhulbahanta found this argument unacceptable, and insisted on withdrawal.

The issue could not be resolved and the two clans engaged in fierce fighting, which lasted for seven years. The British colonial government tried hard to stop this war. It exacted fines, and brought the clans together for peace settlements. Government forces patrolled the border, and even attacked both sides on occasion. None of these measures was successful. Almost every week saw the death of clan members, or raids on each other's livestock.

In 1954 almost all the Habarje'lo subgroups began driving down south beyond the border. This widened the battle front, and the Dhulbahanta began to feel that the clan's very survival was at stake.

In December 1955, elders of the western Dhulbahanta and Habarje'lo subgroups, under pressure from the government, met and agreed a comprehensive peace settlement. But less than one month later, the Habarje'lo infiltrated deep into the Dhulbahanta settlement, and attacked hamlets just 15 km north of the main Dhulbahanta town of Las Anod.

By 1957, the government was growing impatient. More importantly, both sides were war-weary and anxious to reach a settlement. After the loss of thousands of lives, a long process of negotiation between the two sides finally established peace.

Although successions of wars have not been uncommon among the Somali clans, the Hargaga conflict was exceptionally bloody. The Dhulbahanta were physically and psychologically defeated, and their peace treaty meant conceding to the Habarje'lo large parts of their richest land, together with many wells.

CHAPTER THREE

Ancient Rivalry

> Pastoralists can have an enormous influence on the upkeep and maintenance of the farmers' fields. The yields of a plot of land can be improved if, during the dry season, a pastoralist brings his animals to stay in the field. This practice benefits each group. The fertility of the land is improved by the animals' excrement, whilst the animals are well nourished by the stems of the crops.
> *Gawa Assoumane, farmer, Niger*

Sahelian pastoralists have always competed to some extent with farmers, both for land and for water. The relationship can be mutually beneficial, especially if the balance between people and resources is healthy. Different groups have found ways of reconciling their potentially conflicting interests, as the following story from Chadian journalist **Mahamat Hissène** illustrates.

Cows versus sorghum
by Mahamat Hissène

Once upon a time, according to a legend told in some Chadian herders' clans, a bull travelling to Lake Fitri took with him all the calves from the hamlet where he had spent the previous season. The calves' owners followed their animals' tracks and found them by Lake Fitri (see map in Chapter Four, p70). This is how they discovered this Garden of Eden, where water and fresh grass are available all year round. The practice of nomadism is said to have begun with this incident.

The legend goes on to say that there was already in Fitri a man who grew sorghum. The Boulala people, who live in villages nestling around Lake Fitri, take this as evidence that they were the first to settle in the area. The Boulala today cultivate millet in the lake bed and *berbéré* (water sorghum) on the areas covered by the annual flood waters of the lake. They are mainly fishermen, breeding oxen and goats as a sideline.

Modus vivendi

Until the early 1960s, when Chad became independent, the date of the nomads' arrival in Fitri during the dry season was determined in agreement with the Boulala sultan. Leaders from the herding districts would send emissaries to the sultan to inform him of their people's wish to "go down" to the lake. He then consulted with his subjects on the state of their crops. If the millet fields had not yet been harvested or if the *berbéré* transplantation was still under way, the sultan could ask herders to postpone their arrival by a few weeks or even a month.

The sultan always asked the farmers to prepare corridors or routes through which the animals could pass on their way to the lakeside grass. Moussa, a Boulala who still remembers those days, recalls nostalgically that in return for such consideration herders respected the Fitri customary authorities and traditions: "They knew how to restrain their animals and did not stray into forbidden areas."

However, Abou Alkhali, an Arab herder, recalls a less harmonious relationship: "It was impossible to control the cows completely when they went through those lush fields; sometimes, an animal would break away from the herd and pull out some leaves or stems." This was, according to him, an ideal excuse for the farmers to confiscate some oxen and ask for compensation.

Two elderly Boulala now living in the Chadian capital, N'Djamena, insist upon the friendliness that used to prevail between families of herders and farmers, even between Boulala villagers and Arab clans. The mutual confidence was such that many farming families would entrust their cattle to the nomads, who would take them north with their own herds and continue caring for them after their return to Fitri. At the time of the dry-season reunion, herders would often pay their respects to their sedentary "partners" by bringing them butter or milk. Farmers, too, gave produce from their fields—millet, groundnuts, sesame. For certain clans, this alliance went even deeper: some Arabs came directly under the sultan's jurisdiction.

Jeremy Hartley/Panos Pictures

Lake Fitri in the dry season. Deteriorating environmental conditions are straining relationships between farmers and herders.

The Boulala and the Arabs agree on one point: the herders today are charged no duty for their stay by Lake Fitri. This situation seems so natural to everyone that any query as to its origins causes real puzzlement. It may have arisen from the fact that before colonisation both groups were under the authority of the Ouaddai kingdom.

With the advent of modern administration, Arab herders pay their tax and tithe to their local district leader in their northern territory. They submit, however, to the decisions of the Boulala sultan and his lieutenants over any straightforward policing of offences. In cases of theft, fighting or damage to fields, these traditional Boulala authorities pass judgement and fix fines. The Arab herders' district leaders rarely visit Lake Fitri, probably to avoid any potential clash of authority with the local Boulala chiefs.

Government intervention

> Today pastoralism is an impossible activity because there is no rain and no grass. There are no pure pastoralists left in this area: everyone now has land which they farm, in addition to keeping animals. Animals deprived of all good grazing tend to go in the fields and cause damage. This has created a dangerous state of affairs between the farmers and the pastoralists.
> *Sadou Iboun, farmer and pastoralist, Burkina Faso*

> Years ago relations between us [the farmers] and the pastoralists were cordial and built on reciprocal trust. We would entrust our cows to the pastoralists who would guard them for us....Today, relations between the farmers and pastoralists have deteriorated and we no longer respect pastoralists enough to let them care for our animals.
> *Four farmers, Burkina Faso*

The mutually accommodating relationship around Lake Fitri described by Mahamat Hissène is becoming rarer, as settled farming in the Sahel has expanded into traditional grazing areas and pastoralists feel themselves to be increasingly under threat.

Governments, both colonial and African, have not often taken a neutral stance in the relationship between pastoralism and agriculture. In general, they have actively favoured agriculture in their law-making, development priorities and financial planning. Agriculture is seen to be more modern and productive, and believed to serve the interests of government more easily, as production can be directed towards, for example, cash crops for export. Governments seek to consolidate and increase their control over their territories, and have a stake in encouraging the increase in numbers, wealth and attachment to the state of settled farmers, who are easier than wandering nomads to integrate into the orbit of state control.

In Sahelian countries, capital accumulation has invaded traditional subsistence economies. The first capitalist development in modern times was brought by colonial governments and settlers, who established infrastructure and attitudes which supported settled cultivation. Once these had been created, a momentum kept capital investment bound up largely with settled farming. Nevertheless, although the government does not favour pastoral production systems, animals still represent individual wealth. Many Sahelians invest any surplus wealth they have in livestock. This has led to the relatively recent phenomenon of numerous pastoralists becoming paid herders, looking after the capital asset of the new absentee livestock owners: mainly landowners, civil servants and businessmen.

Two other factors tending towards the breakdown of traditional pastoralism are improved animal health, which has upset the balance between herds and pasture, and the deterioration of the environment, which has forced farmers to abandon exhausted or eroded soils and to cultivate ever more marginal, and formerly pastoral, land. Drought, of course, exacerbates the situation.

Governments are only just beginning to realise the seriousness of the problem, and to reconsider the dismissive attitudes they have held for so long towards pastoralists. Senegalese journalist **Babacar Touré**, editor of *Sud Hebdo* newspaper in Dakar, examines the background to the situation in Senegal.

Prejudice and policy
by Babacar Touré

> **Conflicts between farmers and pastoralists are common, but in my opinion it is always the pastoralist who provokes them. Pastoralists have been known to drive up to 30 cows into a field. If the farmer tries to object or ask for an explanation, the pastoralist hits him!**
> *Sayanna Hatho, farmer, Niger*

> **The villagers and the animal raisers used to quarrel a bit, but nothing like they do today. There is far too much hate in people's hearts today. In the old days, when the animals damaged a field, we used to send the menfolk down to check the damaged area, and then its owner would punish the victim. But nowadays it's all done by force, because people no longer have pity in their hearts for others.**
> *Diangou Kante, farmer, Senegal*

In 1964, the recently independent government of Senegal introduced a new law on national property, which increased the already existing discrimination against nomadic herders. It decreed that land should belong to those who "put it to profitable use"—which was usually understood to mean farmers, as opposed to pastoralists. Through this 1964 law, and following administrative reforms introduced in 1972, management of land-tenure was transferred from the traditional chieftains to public authorities. Local communities, represented by rural councils, gained authority over most of the land in their area.

In 1973 drought struck, and it lasted several years. What had until then been momentary tensions between groups with opposing interests deteriorated into real conflicts, sometimes with fatal results. Such events were hardly likely to temper the long-held prejudices against the Fulani ethnic group in Senegal, who are mostly pastoralists and were thought by the farmers of other ethnic groups, particularly Wolof, to be "bloodthirsty and careless of human life".

One story tells of a Fulani who burst out laughing in the police cell where he was being held after chopping up an adversary. What was so funny? "It's dreadful how cowardly a Wolof can be. Did you know the guy was farting when I cut his throat!" The Fulani may have an exaggerated reputation, but it is worth tracing the roots of this ill-feeling between farmers and herders.

It stems partly from a fundamental difference in outlook summed up well in this Wolof saying: "When a Fulani turns to farming, he has lost all hope in life, for he sees in each tussock of grass such a quantity of milk that every stalk cut by a plough seems like litres of white liquid spilled on the earth." From the Fulani point of view, each new area of land cleared for agriculture means loss of pasture. One can understand that herders in the Ferlo region will always see large-scale farmers as the agents of their misfortune and dishonour.

State "favouritism"

According to Ibrahim Dia, Senegalese Deputy Director of Livestock, until the French colonial administration introduced deep wells in the Ferlo region (centre-north and northern Senegal, see map in Chapter Five, p84), the herders "lived in symbiosis" with nature, which provided them with abundantly wooded and shrubby steppes and lush seasonal or permanent pastures. This common patrimony, "open to all", was managed "without any clashes or deterioration, for centuries".

Then came the French land-holding code of 1830 instituting western-style tenure, which favoured private ownership and settled use of land, ie agriculture. Senegal gained independence in 1960,

UNEP

Herders of livestock are often blamed for degrading the land, but some research shows that pastoralism is a more efficient system of land use than large-scale agriculture.

but the new state moved even further in the same direction and took no measures to prevent conflict between farmers and pastoralists over the fundamental need for land. The law-makers of the young state had one concern: to lay the basis for an increase in agricultural production. They concentrated especially on groundnuts, the cash mono-crop established by French colonialism. Promoters of groundnut production, more than any other sector, enjoyed the state's favours.

The government did not think of agriculture as an ensemble of activities which included crops and livestock, despite the fact that today livestock contributes around 30% of the Gross Domestic Product of the rural sector. Increasingly, agricultural specialists are denouncing what they consider to be an "oversight" by the law-makers, and point out that in the long term it is probably herders who make more "profitable use" of land than the farmers, since animals convert vegetation into meat for less investment than agriculture demands.

The best relationship with the big farmers which herders can hope for is one of dependence. These farmers exploit the state's "favouritism" towards them, demonstrating a better grasp of reality than the government's. Farmers recognise the importance of manure for soil fertility. Relatively prosperous peasants make contracts with livestock-owners, who are paid in various ways to graze, or enclose their herds between seasons, in harvested fields.

The law and the farmers' prejudices are justified partly by the assumption that livestock impoverish the land. How far is this true? The debate is an old one, and each side can provide supporting evidence. Recently the debate intensified: those who claim that the Sahelian area of Senegal (a good half of the country) is doomed to continual degradation of its environment, or even total desertification, are being called upon to qualify their pessimism. The Ecological Monitoring Centre (CSE) in Dakar, which has carried out surveys from the air and on the ground, has come to the conclusion that some "alarmist statements" concerning the degree of degradation of the pastoral ecosystems in the area should be modified.

In the area concerned, which covers the regions of Saint Louis, Louga and Diourbel (109,000 sq km), some 4 million cattle, goats, sheep, donkeys and horses share the rangelands with camels. The largest camel herds come from Mauritania, and follow seasonal transhumance patterns theoretically regulated by official agreements between Senegal and Mauritania. These agreements, however, have never stopped the herders from the north from coming into conflict with both Senegalese herders and farmers.

So-called excessive pressure on the ecosystems by livestock is regarded by many as a major factor in desertification. Supporters of this theory cite the upsurge in herd size following the return of the rains in 1985 and as a result of Senegal's veterinary health policy, which has led to the eradication of rinderpest and anthrax.

Prejudices about livestock abound. The camel's urine is supposed to be so acid that it kills off plants; its feet are said to be so heavy that they break up the soil and reduce it to dust, which is then carried away by the wind, along with the humus, leading to loss of fertility. Furthermore, the camel eats everything in its path, right up to the tops of the trees. Goats, too, are supposed to ravage vegetation. A reputedly finicky eater, the goat has a taste for buds, thus preventing plant reproduction.

Veterinarians and botanists refute such theories. Goats are the most successful of Sahelian animals, able to digest a wide range of plants and to reproduce at a rapid rate. Camels are the animals best suited to dry regions, even if they are slow breeders, while cattle thrive best on wetter grasslands.

Increasing pressure

Not surprisingly, the herder of the 1990s who tries to maintain the migration patterns of his ancestors finds himself "trespassing" in cultivated areas. As lands are fast being given over to groundnut or cereal production, and as such decisions are not always publicised, a herder who returns to a region after a two-year absence may soon find his old way barred.

According to research undertaken by Oussouby Touré, a sociologist at the CSE, "climatic crises have produced not only social imbalances, but also appreciable ecological disruption in the river zone of north Senegal, where environmental degradation is becoming ever more worrying". When animals need to move south or east, they find in their path large areas of land stripped of trees and wild grasses. They cannot take a step without walking into a field. Agriculture confronts herding—and the herder finds that the law is biased against him.

After the drought-ridden decade of the 1970s, the government became aware of the seriousness of periodic clashes between rural communities. Senegalese herders welcomed the decree of March 1980, which dealt with the organisation of livestock movements and set the conditions for use of pastureland. The document distinguishes between "all natural open spaces traditionally used for grazing animals" and other types of pasture. There was no proposal to return to livestock the areas already given over to groundnuts and millet, but there was a statement that henceforward "the status of all or part of the natural pastures can only be altered following a detailed study leading to the establishment of a formal statement of change of status". The subsequent provisions laid such stress on the need to protect areas of pasture that more than one herder thought his dreams were coming true.

Ten years later, there is no sign of the decree being put into practice. And since 1985, Senegalese rural communities have had to face up to a new reality. Because of "structural adjustment" of the economy, the government has launched a new agricultural policy based on empowerment of peasants, on disengagement of the state, on phasing out the parastatal companies which formerly controlled most aspects of agricultural production and marketing, and on withdrawal of subsidies on fertiliser and other inputs.

From now on producers will need to sow larger areas in order to make a profit. Large-scale farmers, as a result of their influence with the public authorities, go on clearing land and changing its status, to the dismay of those for whom livestock is everything.

Whenever a piece of land becomes less productive, farmers move on, preferably to an area which has lain fallow for decades and which can be "put to profitable use", thanks to animal manure. The police often have to intervene to settle disputes and to oblige herders to respect a land-tenure code which in practice has rarely considered them.

Herders bitterly resent the forced "expropriation" of land for agriculture, and have even become nostalgic about the colonial era. Many attest to the fact that "formerly, a herder could move around all day with his animals without meeting any other herds in the bush. Now, if you tell a farmer not to settle in a certain place because it is your customary pasture, he will say that you cannot own the bush—and the administration will take his side." In a dispute between a local farmer and a herder over such pastureland, the herder is considered to be a "foreigner". Men without land, herders are permanently on the move, seeking pasture.

Is there a solution?

> **There was a day when the Peulh [Fulani] knew how to respect us and when you found them in your field they would offer you an animal as a way of apologising, whereas now they are ready to quarrel with us. That is all the more true since the harvests are no longer as good as they were.**
> *Siga Gassama, farmer, Senegal*

Are pastoralism and agriculture condemned to a future of ever-increasing conflict? Not necessarily. For one thing, there is mounting evidence that the desertification which has spread over the Sahelian region during the past two decades may not be permanent. According to the CSE, which has compared the years 1987-89 to earlier drought years, there is evidence that not only is degradation "not irreversible", but regrowth of vegetation is apparent and the bulk of the wild seed-stock remains dormant in the soil. Furthermore, findings show that the pastoral area is generally undergrazed in years of average rainfall, and that pressure from animals is much greater in the agricultural zone.

Could these findings, in the event of a recovery of the rains, be the key to a solution of rural conflicts? In practice, it is very unlikely that this single factor would lead to any change. Only the enforcement of a just and balanced law of land-tenure will be able to change the basic relationship between herders and farmers from conflict to cooperation.

Pressure from all sides

In east Sudan, pastoralists face difficulties from three directions: from the expansion of mechanised farming; from the influx of refugees from Ethiopia and Eritrea; and from thousands of bandits or *faloul*, an aspect explored in more detail in Chapter Six. Drought and famine have added to these three problems.

Thousands of Sudanese herders, unable to take the usual route to survival by moving south, have had to accept a sedentary lifestyle, earning wages as labourers for the very farmers and merchants whose activities and political strength have contributed to their situation. Many nomadic tribes have been affected, such as the Shukriya, the Rashaida, the Hadendawa and the Beni Amer. **Berhane Woldegabriel**, an Eritrean journalist based in Khartoum, tells the story of one tribe: the Lahawin.

Pastoralists cornered
by Berhane Woldegabriel

The Lahawin, like virtually every Muslim ethnic group in Sudan, trace their ancestry back to the Arabian peninsula and the Prophet Mohamed. Unlike some other Muslim ethnic groups in Sudan, who have their own dialects, the Lahawin speak Arabic. They came to east Sudan little more than a century ago, from Kordofan in the west of the country.

The paramount chief of the Lahawin, 60-year-old Sheikh El Zein, now lives with growing numbers of his followers in a permanent village, Magatae, between the towns of Showak and Khash el Girba. He says that his grandparents moved to the east in

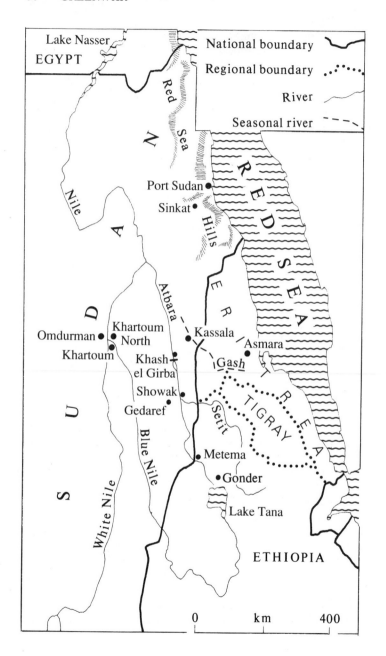

Lake Nasser
EGYPT

National boundary
Regional boundary
River
Seasonal river

Red Sea

N

Nile

RED SEA

Port Sudan
Sinkat

Hills

A

Atbara

E R

Omdurman
Khartoum North
Khartoum
Khash el Girba
Showak
Gedaref

Kassala
Asmara
Gash

D

T

I

R

E

A

Setit

TIGRAY

Blue Nile

Metema
Gonder

S

White Nile

Lake Tana

U

ETHIOPIA

0   km   400

order to escape the heavier taxation in the west. His brother and deputy, Ahmed, disagrees. According to him, the 800 km journey from Kordofan to the Gedaref area was made because of one horse. El Tom, the chief of the Baggara, the powerful cattle-herding tribe of west Sudan, demanded the personal horse of the subdued chief of the Lahawin. The vanquished Lahawin chief then left the scene of his humiliation, and led his tribe to live in the Gedaref area.

Though disagreeing on the history of their arrival, the brothers concur over the present size of their tribe in the east, estimating it at about 600,000. Probably encouraged by the vastness of their country (the largest in Africa), and by the sparse population, Sudanese pastoralists maintained the tradition that land is communal and should not be privatised. Unaware of government decrees, they believed that the land of their forefathers was theirs. In law, however, all land in Sudan belongs to the government, and individuals or institutions must secure short- or long-term leases, which may last as long as 30 years, depending on land use. Other groups have benefited from this law, such as the West African peoples from Chad and Nigeria, who have occupied lands by the river banks and beds. They have more "modern" views about land-holding than most of the Sudanese pastoralists, who have never registered land in their name.

Tractor cultivation

The British administration introduced mechanised rainfed farming in the Gedaref area in the 1930s, to provide food for the allied forces that fought against Mussolini's Italian colonial army in Eritrea and Ethiopia. The government of independent Sudan carried on the policy of clearing vast tracts of forest land for agriculture, establishing a special department of the Ministry of Agriculture and Natural Resources: the Mechanised Farming Corporation (MFC).

During the 1970s, there was optimism about Sudan's prospects. A vast land, well-endowed with fertile soil, sufficient rainfall an irrigation waters, as well as with skilled human resources, it seeme to have all the ingredients to produce enough food not only for itse but also for neighbouring Arab countries. Its proximity to 1 oil-rich, food-importing countries in the Gulf was a comparat advantage. Agricultural banks gave generous loans to "enlightened", who were mainly retired government offici merchants and some rich farmers. In a hasty and ambitious ver

to turn Sudan into the "bread basket" of the Middle East, the MFC distributed 400-hectare (1,000 feddan) or 600-hectare plots. The average area registered per landholder was about 8,900 hectares.

Clearing forest for farms

To make way for this large-scale farming, thousands of hectares of forest land were cleared. Wildlife, including lions, elephants, leopards and hyenas, which had already been moving southwards since the Italo-British wars in the early 1940s, suffered further incursions into their habitat. And as tractor cultivation expanded, it depleted the pastoralists' traditional grazing grounds.

"The tractor is the culprit," stated Sheikh El Zein of the Lahawin. Figures do show that the number of tractors in Sudan doubled in 10 years, from 8,767 in 1974-76 to over 17,000 in 1983-88 [1]. "Before the advent of the tractor to our area, we used to get our *eish* [which means both bread and *dura* (sorghum), the staple cereal] from our small-scale shifting cultivation," lamented Sheikh El Zein. "Now our land is lost to the owners of farms. Worse still, now that they have started to own cattle themselves, they do not sell us straw anymore." Such feelings about the destruction which takes place in the name of development are not new. "When the Khash el Girba dam was built in 1958, it was referred to by the Lahawin as *the year of cutting trees*," reflected one of Sheikh El Zein's fellow villagers.

Memories of the dam construction sparked off talk among the villagers of another pressure on the pastoralists: the influx of refugees, an estimated 500,000 from Ethiopia and Eritrea, with whom the Lahawin have to compete for resources and work. The Lahawin resented the fact that the Italian companies in charge of building the dam preferred to hire Eritreans, because they spoke Italian. The refugees had also been given parts of the Lahawin grazing land for settlement, a loss for which the pastoralists say they have not yet received government compensation. The Lahawin also felt that the Eritreans had seriously depleted wood stocks in the area, depriving the Lahawin of building materials and fuelwood: the Eritreans, claimed the Lahawin, do not use charcoal but prefer to cut down trees for firewood.

Competition for land

The MFC had to stop selling plots of agricultural land in 1986, because all the land demarcated for rainfed agriculture had been

used. MFC officials blame regional governments for distributing land outside the demarcated areas. The total area under tractor cultivation in 1986-87 was 2.8 million hectares, of which only about half was within the area demarcated by the MFC. Yet in May 1990 the Sudanese Minister of Agriculture announced that 5.5 million hectares would be mechanically cultivated in 1991. Even the area that receives under 400 mm of rainfall per year has been put under mechanised agriculture, which is a risky investment.

Mechanised farming has eaten up huge tracts of land, leaving little for the pastoralists. "Land for agriculture was distributed on the assumption that unregistered land is empty," said an MFC employee, who wishes to remain anonymous. Traditional Lahawin grazing lands, which had covered vast areas of Kassala province from Gedaref to the borders of Ethiopia and Eritrea, were taken over. Rainfall there ranges from 400 mm up to 800 mm yearly.

The activities of the big farmers have affected fundamentally the lives of hundreds of thousands of pastoralists in Kassala province. "Owners of mechanised farms like neither trees nor animals," explained a Shukriya pastoralist living in the Fau area, a view also held by the Lahawin at Magatae. The landowners are town dwellers, living in Gedaref, who care little about research which demonstrates that pastoralism makes more economical use of marginal land than mechanised farming does. Pastoralists who exploit the marginal areas require nothing from the outside except vaccines for their animals. The inputs required by farming, such as fertilisers, diesel and spare parts, have to be imported with hard currency.

"Sales of animal products are an essential source of hard currency in Sudan, being perhaps more than the sum total of the revenue from the rainfed mechanised farms. Although the areas under cultivation are seven times what they were some 20 years ago, the size of harvest per unit area has decreased to less than half," claimed Dr Mohamed Khair Omer, head of the Commission for Refugees' Veterinary Unit. Long-term problems associated with inappropriate techniques and over-intensive farming are becoming clearer, as the declining productivity of the large farms illustrates.

"The law protects rich farmers"

Corridors, made by leaving some plots fallow, are needed for the movement of the nomads and their animals across the mechanised farms. The herds are not granted free passage, and the pastoralist has to compensate to the landowner for any grass eaten. This is usually cheaper than buying grain but not always. Sheikh El Zein says that in 1989 one of his subjects, Ahmed Wad Ali, paid 30,000 Sudanese pounds (US$6,683) because his animals, mainly camels and sheep, damaged some crops as they were travelling north.

Awad El Karim, one of Sheikh El Zein's nine sons and an employee of the Forestry Unit of Showak, cited an incident from his personal experience. To his delight, he once caught a farmer who had just illegally cut down many trees to prepare some land for his agricultural machinery. The court fined the farmer 167,000 Sudanese pounds (about US$37,204) but he appealed. Three years later, the case has still not been finalised. At Maharagat, near Showak, another farmer was charged with cutting trees and fined 7,000 Sudanese pounds (about US$1,559). He too appealed and the case is still pending.

One powerful farmer even appropriated a complete *haffir* (water-hole), which had initially been dredged by the North Gedaref Council to cater for pastoralists who pass through Kasamour area, northwest of Showak. The rural council officer in Showak decided in favour of the farmer, on the grounds that the *haffir* was located on his plot of land, in spite of the fact that the rural council had virtually abandoned the *haffir* and that it had been rehabilitated by the Lahawin, who had contributed money and rented a caterpillar tractor to repair it. The case became more serious when some frustrated young Lahawin men took the law into their own hands, and beat up the rich farmer, as well as a policeman who had tried to stop the animals from drinking at the *haffir*.

"Although it is usually one rich farmer or merchant against an entire pastoral community," said the Sheikh's brother Ahmed, "it is the rich man who wins. As far as I can see, the laws are either made for them or by them."

Governments have made some attempts to compensate the Lahawin for the loss of their traditional lands. Some Lahawin were given *hawashas* (plots of land) in the irrigation scheme at New Halfa, which was primarily designed to accommodate the Halfawin who lost their home town on the border with Egypt when the Aswan dam was built in the 1950s. During the first few years of the scheme, members of the army had to guard the irrigated area against pastoralist trespassers, who found it difficult to accept or adjust to the new government venture. Lahawin children still sing of the "cruel and bitter" white men who built the Khash el Girba dam.

As large-scale farming eats into traditional grazing land, herders and animals are squeezed into smaller and smaller areas.

They sing of malaria and other negative consequences of irrigation schemes, of the eviction of their animals from the sugar and cotton plantations and of how their people's natural pattern of movement had to change.

Intertribal conflicts

"When the land started to shrink before our eyes, those of us who used to live in harmony started to grumble at each other over water," said the Sheikh's son Awad El Karim.

Haffirs along the pastoralists' stock routes date from the days of the British administration. Over time, not only did the pressure of animals on each *haffir* increase, as farming took over pasture land, but many of the *haffirs* also fell into disrepair. Some of those that were rehabilitated became the "exclusive property" of particular nomadic clans. This has given rise to several conflicts, mostly armed, between pastoralist tribes.

"The Rashaida are the most heavily armed pastoralists in eastern Sudan, if not in the whole country. During the 1983-84 drought they received considerable amounts of money from Saudi Arabia. Many of them bought modern automatic guns and fast Land Cruisers," recounted police captain Hassan Kashaba, head of the border section of Kassala province in Gedaref, in May 1990.

In an attempt to play down the increasing bloody skirmishes and discourage a glamorous or macho image of violence, such information is suppressed. However, the police captain admitted that there are what he called "repeated incidents" of intertribal rivalry among the Shukriya, Rashaida, Kunana and Lahawin over water for animals.

Drought

How far do successive years of drought contribute to the permanent desertification of land? Drought certainly accelerates land degradation and its impact is likely to be more severe in areas already under environmental stress. But the Sahelian environment, while more "fragile" than ecosystems in temperate or tropical zones, does have its own effective recovery mechanisms. Plant, animal and insect life are well adapted to the Sahelian climate, with its extremes and swift changes. The ecosystem is well able to take advantage of short periods of rainfall and to cope with less favourable times by, for example, long periods of dormancy. In many drought-stricken areas, vegetation reappears and the land recovers once rain falls, after even very extended dry periods. There are other significant causes of the degradation of land, which often has a less dramatic appearance than land affected by drought. Climatic change may be one cause, but others are human activities such as farming and cutting trees, processes which are more susceptible to modification than is the climate.

What is clear is that drought intensifies competition for resources, and magnifies social inequalities. Small farmers and the poorer pastoralists are the first to feel the effects. As water sources dry up, the pastoralists' animals die or have to be sold at depressed prices. In the longer term, this loss of stock reduces the herders to poverty. It takes years to rebuild herds, if indeed it is ever possible. At the same time, drought makes farmers more protective of their land and water sources, increasing the tension between them and the herders. The next writer, **Zeremariam Fre**, an Eritrean academic specialising in pastoralist issues, looks at an area where drought has forced more and more pastoralist groups to survive on the same limited resources.

Intercommunal conflict
by Zeremariam Fre

Prior to the introduction of mechanised farming, only Beni Amer and Sudanese pastoralists utilised the grazing land of the area between Setit and Gash (see map in Chapter Eight, p135). Since 1950, however, many new groups and their herds have started coming there, as their own traditional grazing lands have disappeared.

At present there are three nomadic, two semi-nomadic and four semi-sedentary groups using these resources for all or part of the year, especially during the dry seasons. Between 200 and 300 nomads, mostly Beni Amer from northern Eritrea, annually bring in an estimated 40,000-80,000 cattle, plus 5,000 sheep and goats. Other cattle are brought by local herders and semi-sedentary groups, and there are additional cattle owned by wealthy farmers who hire the Beni Amer to keep them.

Increased mechanised farming schemes, and the relatively recent arrival of some Ethiopian highland groups (Wolgait and Tsegede) along the eastern and southern fringes of the area, have jeopardised the welfare of the Beni Amer more than that of any other nomadic people using the area.

The Beni Amer have little choice but to attempt to continue to use their traditional migration routes into the central and southern parts of the Setit-Gash area, for there are water and feed shortages nearer their home base. Recently, it has become increasingly difficult for them to find grazing, because the grasslands they once relied upon are now largely farmed, and the lands between the east of this area and the highlands, and south of the Tekeze River, are used by Hamasian, Wolgait and Tsegede herdsmen and are not available to the Beni Amer. Beni Amer cattle are not allowed to move south of the Tekeze River until after the southern crop harvest is over. The Beni Amer have to rely heavily on crop residues, and then try to avoid areas where they are not welcome.

This is not easy, because almost all farmers prefer the Beni Amer herds to stay off their land. Some even burn the crop residues and the remaining grassland to discourage the pastoralists. One particular factor is the conviction held by farmers that noxious *striga* weeds are brought onto their land by migrating cattle, a suspicion for which there is some circumstantial evidence. In fields which are already infested with *striga*, seeds drop among the sorghum and other plants. Migrating cattle browsing in the crop residues eat the seeds along with the fodder. Later, the cattle move to weed-free areas and deposit the seeds in their manure. Seeds can also be carried in mud clinging to the animals' hooves.

And as if to close off the only remaining safety-valve for the Beni Amer, if they attempt to avoid the cropland by moving eastward, they are subject to reprisals from armed Hamasian and highland herdsmen [2].

CHAPTER FOUR

The Role of the State

Sahelian governments, and the international donors who support their policies. are only now beginning to acknowledge the dangers of neglecting the tensions caused by intensifying competition for resources. In particular, many governments have not yet taken effective steps to compensate pastoralists for their lost lands, or to resolve other conflicts in just and long-lasting ways. This section describes one example where government neglect of pastoralists' grievances eventually led to violent protest.

The Tuareg demand recognition

The Tuareg, or Tamashek, are one group whose anger at an inadequate government response to their situation following the 1984-85 drought, and frustration in 1990 at their lack of political voice and power, turned to violence.

Tuareg pastoralists are indigenous to three African countries: northeastern Mali, central and northern Niger, and Algeria, on the northern side of the Sahara. Tuareg is an Arabic word meaning "the abandoned of God". Because of these negative connotations, the Tuareg call themselves the *Kel Tamashek*, the people who speak Tamashek.

After the drought of 1984-85, several thousand Tuareg from Mali and Niger sought alternative pasture on the northern side of the Sahara, in Algeria. The International Fund for Agricultural Development (IFAD), established in 1977 after the UN World Food Conference, joined forces with the governments of Algeria, Mali and Niger to resettle the group back in Mali. After almost three years

National boundary

River

•2022 Spot height, metres above s.l.

LIBYA

ALGERIA

Aïr
Mountains
•2022

MALI

NIGER

Gao

Menaka

Tillia

Tchin Tabaraden

CHAD

Niger

Niamey

Lake Chad

NIGERIA

0   km   400

of discussion, implementation began in February 1990. At the same time, it appears that thousands more Tuareg returned to Niger from Libya, following promises of reintegration made by the Nigerien head of state, Ali Seibou. No wells had been maintained or dug for several years in the Aïr mountains in Niger, where many Tuareg live. So they were directed to provisional camps around the town of Tchin Tabaraden.

It is not entirely clear what went wrong, but within a few months in early 1990 groups of Tuareg were complaining bitterly. The food aid they should have received through the Niger government had apparently not arrived. Three or four Tuareg aged about 20 decided to occupy the gendarmerie (police post) at Tchin Tabaraden. They wanted to draw attention to the conditions in which they were living, still waiting for the promised relief food which they suspected had been stolen. In the fight which followed, one of them got hold of a gendarme's gun; two gendarmes and a prisoner were killed.

The young men fled into the desert with their weapons, taking a forestry guard as hostage. The government sent the army after them, and the arrival of the soldiers seemed to have caused panic in the town. People ran away into the desert and small villages around Tchin Tabaraden.

It was still the dry season in Niger, when pastoralists have to water their animals at least once every two days. The Tuareg claim that the military occupied the water points in the area and shot at pastoralists as they approached. They claim that the military encircled camps, raped women, stripped elders naked and killed young people. According to a report published in France, the worst horrors took place at Tillia, a village 50 km from Tchin Tabaraden, where pastoralists claimed that many were massacred with machine guns [1]. They alleged that children were shot in front of their parents to encourage them to reveal where arms were hidden.

It was three weeks before the army withdrew. The official figure was 70 dead but Tuareg estimates put it at 200-300 men, women and children.

Conflict spreads

It was no surprise that the events in Niger had an impact in Mali. The border between the two countries, created during colonial times, has always been artificial for pastoralists, and the Tuareg have no great respect for this political boundary, which runs through the centre of their traditional grazing areas.

A month after the army had withdrawn in Niger, Malian staff from the non-governmental organisation World Vision, based in the small northeastern Malian town of Menaka, were travelling north when a lone Tuareg gunman stopped their two jeeps. Twenty other Tuareg then surrounded the vehicles. One Malian was beaten; others were shaken up. They were forced back into the cars, and taken to the small town of Inkadawane, which was almost completely deserted.

The Tuareg continued south with the vehicles to Menaka. Early the next morning, they attacked the gendarmerie, where 13 people were killed (mainly gendarmes and soldiers), and ransacked the compounds of two aid agencies, destroying eight vehicles, looting warehouses, offices and living quarters, and stealing approximately US$27,000 worth of spare parts and diesel, and six vehicles, before returning to Inkadawane.

They explained that they were fighting for the entire Tuareg pastoralist people, who had been oppressed in the past by the French and were now being oppressed by the Malian government. Nonetheless, the rebellion was not widely supported, although it did provide the opportunity for some intellectuals in the capital, Bamako, to protest about the existing political system.

Within a few days, increased army activity was reported in the Gao area. Over the next few weeks, a number of Tuareg were arrested, and explosives which aid agencies and the government hydraulics department were using in their well construction programmes were confiscated.

On 15 July, a rebel attack was reported on Tarkin, 120 km from Gao, with three people killed. Less than a week later, fighting took place in the major town of Gao itself, with automatic weapons and hand-grenades. Gendarmes in Gao said that the rebels were well-equipped and well-organised. Stories circulating locally alleged that Libya had trained the Tuareg. Some Tuareg stated that one of their objectives was to fight for a Saharan state for pastoralist peoples, stretching from the Atlantic coast across to Chad.

Executions

In late July and mid-August 1990, two public executions of Tuareg were carried out in Gao by the Malian government. Those executed were charged as "rebels carrying guns".

There was a strong reaction from the government in Niger to the limited French press coverage of the incidents. The Minister of Communications in Niger, Khamed Abdoulaye, is the only Tuareg minister. In a long interview with *Le Sahel*, the government newspaper, he stressed the fact that the pastoralists' lifestyle meant that they had no effective participation in the decision-making processes of the country. The rare moments of contact between the authorities and the people of the pastoral zones took place when taxes were being collected, or when the pastoralists were brought out to welcome a figure of authority from the capital city.

According to the minister: "The only contact between [pastoralist] people at the grassroots and the administration is through the gendarmes, the republican guard, who mostly behave as if they were on conquered territory, and because of this they symbolise pure violence in the eyes of the population."

He therefore proposed "the transfer as soon as possible of all the administrators, ministry staff, guards and gendarmes who symbolise violence. In their place, we must put men who are open to dialogue....In this way the [pastoralist] populations will feel confident, will feel themselves to be involved with everything that contributes to regional life."

He also heavily criticised traditional pastoralist chiefs and said that "it would be desirable to begin a process of which the aim would be to allow the people to choose new chiefs who have popular support. In short, to encourage mechanisms of popular participation [2]."

Although the immediate response of the Malian and Niger governments was to use force to suppress these Tuareg protests, it appears that the outbursts have encouraged a search for a more long-term solution. In January 1991, the Malian government and the rebels agreed a cease-fire, which included a degree of autonomy for the regions of Mali involved in the rebellion. It may also result in decentralised control of part of the national rural development budget [3]. The Tuareg are not alone in demanding greater participation. Over 100 people were killed by government forces in Bamako in pro-democracy demonstrations which preceded the government's fall in March 1991.

Government intervention

In some cases, rather than suppressing conflict, intervention by the state encourages it. Governments can use existing or potential intercommunal conflict to undermine and weaken groups which they do not favour, or which they feel to be a political threat.

Nhial Bol Aken, a southern Sudanese journalist based in Khartoum and currently writing for *Sudanow* magazine, describes

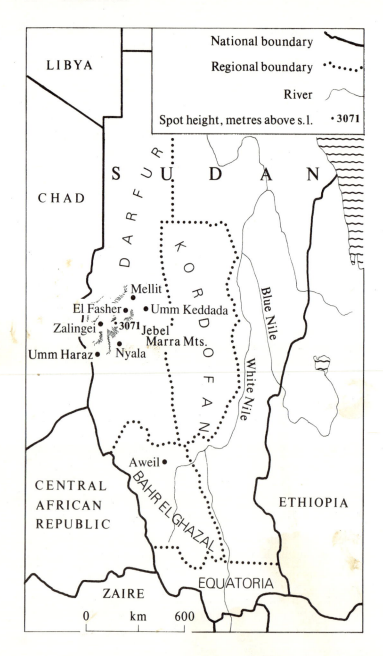

how government support for one group in the intercommunal war in west Sudan has perpetuated and heightened the level of violence. The conflict is less well-known internationally than the major north-south civil war in Sudan, but it is devastating the region. Herders of Arabic origin and settled farmers of black African descent, already suffering the effects of drought, have been fighting for many years. In this particular case, government support has gone to the herders because this has apparently served the purpose of increasing the political dominance of the Arab community throughout Sudan.

Violence fuelled by the state
by Nhial Bol Aken

The population of the province is about 5 million people. The native Fur and other non-Arab tribes represent 60% of the population, and are African Sahara tribes with strong blood relations to West African tribes. The Fur tribe is the second biggest tribe in Sudan after the Dinkas of the south.

The Fur live mainly in Jebel Marra, Zalingei, Garcilla and Wadi Salish, but some are scattered in northern Darfur. They own 90% of the farming and grazing land. There are other non-Arab tribes such as the Massalit, the Zagawa, the Falata Barti, the Tonjur, the Eringa, the Barno, the Dussja, the Bargo and the Bargi. Almost all these tribes originated from West Africa, but settled in Darfur before the First World War. They include both farmers and nomadic pastoralists.

The Arab tribes, which comprise the rest of the region's population, came from the desert areas after the Second World War in search of water and grazing. They live in Darfur, but the majority are pastoralist nomads and move from place to place during the dry

Background: Darfur province
Darfur is a desert and semi-desert province in the extreme west of Sudan which borders Chad, Libya and Central African Republic. It is an important region for trade with these countries. It has always been a remote, feudal area, over which Khartoum has never ruled easily. This was the region where the Mahdi's rebellion against the British started in 1890. There is a history of close links with Libya, and in 1976 Libya backed an attempted coup against President Nimeiri by Sadiq El Mahdi (great-grandson of the Mahdi) .

season. The pastoralist Arab tribes in Darfur are the Baggara, Harbani, Beni Halva, Rezeigat Baggara and Rezeigat Messirya. They do not legally own lands in Darfur.

Ever since their arrival in the province, their relations with the Fur farmers have been strained. The Fur, it is claimed, used to burn all the grazing before the dry season in order to prevent the pastoralists putting their cattle on the fields.

Poor management of natural resources probably magnified the impact of the drought and famine of 1984-85, which badly affected both nomadic pastoralists and traditional farmers. Millions of cattle are reported to have died, as well as countless sheep and goats. Farmers practising traditional agriculture lost 76% of their annual production because of the low rainfall. Since 1985, many areas of farmland have been abandoned as unworkable.

Unrest

Growing population pressure on the limited areas that remain suitable for agriculture has increased the hostility between the competing communities, who have formed themselves into two distinct tribal groups, Arab and African. The Fur in particular drew closer together, to confront the Arab tribes and to prevent them grazing their herds on Fur farmland. Each group illegally armed its tribes and claimed rights of settlement in the region, politically and militarily. Today there is a particularly serious conflict between the Fur and the pastoralist Arab tribe, the Baggara, but clashes take place between the different pastoralist groups as well.

The conflict is limited to grazing and farming rights, there being no religious dispute as there is in south Sudan, and the war zones reflect the geography of the nomadic and farming areas. The situation has been aggravated by the infiltration of weapons, and by the influx of rebels from Chad and Libya. During the conflict which resulted in the overthrow of the Chadian government at the end of 1990, Chadian authorities armed the Beni Halva and Salamat non-Arab tribes, who then attacked both Arabs and Fur. They have destroyed many villages and become professional looters and robbers in the areas around the town of Jebel Marra, attacking on horseback.

The Sudanese government is also responsible for fuelling the violence; it armed some of the Arab tribes, allegedly to gain support for the Umma and National Islamic Front parties. (All political parties have since been banned by the government which came to power in Khartoum in 1989.) The war was allegedly sanctioned by the government because it was in line with its policies of furthering the interests of Arab Sudanese.

It is almost impossible to obtain figures for the total number of deaths but in 1987 alone over 5,000 people were reported killed, mostly from the Fur tribe.

Victims of drought and war

Over 10,000 people were displaced by the war in Darfur in the areas of Jebel Marra, Zalingei, Umm Keddada, Umm Haraz and Mellit. Mohammed Awad, 34, a Rezeigat Baggara Arab tribesman from northern Darfur, is one of many nomadic pastoralists who was forced by drought to move south. Mohammed lost many of his cattle, goats and sheep, and had to abandon his area of El Fasher for southern Darfur in 1976 in search of water and grazing. For four years he lived peacefully alongside the Fur tribes who owned the surrounding farmland.

But in 1980 conflict broke out between the Rezeigat nomads and the Fur farmers. Mohammed explained that the Rezeigat first fought with the Fur when their cattle entered the farms and destroyed the fields. "We quarrelled with the Fur tribes because they prevented us from going further south." The Fur killed two Rezeigat men, looted their cattle and forced them to leave the land. Altogether, the pastoralists lost 50% of the cattle they had driven down to southern Darfur.

Mohammed is now camped in a slum village in Jebel Marra town, where he plans to stay because it is safer. He said he could not return to northern Darfur because the soil there had been damaged by desertification and there was no longer any grazing land.

"Our home was once in the grazing areas, anonymous and nomadic. Everyone enjoyed the privileges of the land." Mohammed's past wealth has gone as his remaining cattle were lost in the war with the Fur: "I lost 100 head of cattle in that conflict. As I am now no longer a nomad, that is the end of my life." Unhappy being a town-dweller, he said he would only resume his normal life as a cattle owner if the "tribal robbery" ceased.

Mohamed Idris, 40, is from the Fur tribe and came from Nyala province to Jebel Marra town. Three years ago, Idris was a farmer in Mellit district, but he moved because of the insecurity there. He said he will go home if the racial conflict between his tribe and the Arab Baggara stops.

Idris has seven children who depend on him but he has no work. His wife Amana left him during the years of drought and famine, and he does not know if she is alive or dead.

In Jebel Marra, he relies on relief food. "It is shameful for us of the Fur tribe to beg food from other people, while our own farms are lying uncultivated in the hands of armed robbers," he complains.

The Fur here are far from happy, because they have lost their original homes and may not be able to return to their settlements. Idris added that some people may not be able to go back to farming work because they have become used to relief food and town life.

Idris claimed that they moved to the town in two groups: the drought and famine victims, and the tribal war victims. The first group from his tribe moved because of the increasing desertification, which led to the 1984-85 famine. He said that this group attempted several times to produce food themselves but the land refused to help them: "They had to flee to towns to become labourers." The other group, which included himself, consisted of people affected by the war between Fur and Arab tribes.

Osman Abaker Adam, 37, is a chief of the Fur tribe, now living in the Nyala camps for the displaced, which are also inhabited by southern Sudanese war victims: "I was forced to leave my home in Mellit and come here three years ago with my children, because of the racial war between us and the Arabs over land rights. I was a farmer, but I abandoned the farm and came to stay here. The Rezeigat Arab tribesmen looted all our cattle and took away the little food we'd grown in 1987. They shot us and burnt our houses after we vacated them. I lost farming lands and 170 bags of *dura* (sorghum). I can truly say I lost all my property in this conflict. My brother was killed by the Arabs and my first wife died on our way here. There are many other farmers like me who fled the war zones. If the government is incapable of resolving the conflict, and does not disarm all the tribes who are carrying illegal weapons, one day we will take the law into our own hands and claim our land rights.

"The Arab Baggara tribes killed many of our people and looted our properties while the government kept quiet, as if it did not know what was happening.

"I would not be happy to stay here for long. I will go back to my own farm lands when the war stops. I am too old to face the difficulties of town life. I would be happier if the authorities gave us a bit of land to cultivate here. Otherwise, I might return home despite the insecurity.

"The people who live in these camps are good people. There are Fur and Arabs, and people from Chad and southern Sudan. They get on with each other because no one has any rights here. They came to this camp in search of food and security. Here, we have no disputes with the Arabs. I am the only chief from Darfur who represents Fur and Arab tribes in the camp, and we live peacefully.

"Our Darfur war could be ended if the Arab tribal leaders and the government accepted that the land belongs to the Fur and the Arabs have no right to settle in Fur areas. We have no problems with the Arab tribes as such, but we are the owners of the land in Darfur, and the Arabs cannot claim any legal land rights. We, the Fur, will fight to separate from Sudan if the government insists on settling the Arab tribes on our lands.

"There is enough land in the Darfur region to be used by both Arab and Fur, as long as the Arabs do not claim ownership. I have good relations with the Arabs, but I cannot allow them to destroy my farms and let them go unpunished because they are pastoralists. The nomadic pastoralists react to us violently if we prevent them from crossing our farms when they are travelling in search of water and grazing land. There will be no solution to this conflict unless the nomads are stopped by law from destroying our farms.

"It is difficult to resolve the conflict now because each group has bought weapons to fight with. These armed tribes have become robbers, looters and highwaymen, who use the gun to stay alive."

Open warfare

For many years, Sudanese governments denied that there was any civil war in Darfur but in 1989 the conflict reached an intensity which could no longer be ignored. In May 1989, the regional government of Darfur admitted that there was racial conflict, and that this had led to armed robbery and tribal unrest throughout the area. It was felt that the fighting, because of the racial element, could threaten national security.

Arab tribes in Jebel Marra had attacked the police station and killed 20 policemen who were attempting to protect the Fur tribe in the villages of Jebel Marra. The governor of Darfur declared the region a "military operation zone" and asked the army to intervene against the warring tribes with their illegal weapons.

This prompted a response from the Defence Minister, and from Sudan's then Prime Minister, Sadiq El Mahdi. Sadiq directed security authorities to review the causes of the Darfur conflict and formed a security committee to accompany him to the region, in order to declare the area a tribal war operation zone. On his return, Sadiq accused neighbouring Chad of providing weapons for the African Fur and of fuelling the conflict. Chad's angry response was to send its army to the Sudanese-Chadian border to confront any military action against it.

In June 1989 the government launched a military operation in the areas inhabited by the northern Rezeigat tribes in Jebel Marra town. Over 3,000 automatic weapons, 140,000 unused hand-grenades and 50,000 rounds of ammunition were seized from the houses of a few individuals. The local courts confiscated all the military hardware but this did not curb the fighting.

It is claimed that Libyan troops of the Islamic Legion have been training certain groups. During 1990, there were nationals from Chad, Central African Republic, Uganda and Kenya on Darfur soil. In addition, until the military coup in Chad at the end of 1990, there were about 23,000 Chadian rebels and refugees. Some of the refugees are living in camps, but an estimated 10,000 were scattered about, living by looting cattle from nomads and settled communities.

Observers feel that the Sudanese government alone cannot solve the tribal war, because as well as the key problems of environmental degradation and the severe and growing limitations on national resources, there are complex links with foreign policies of neighbouring countries.

The danger of armed militias

The government armed and institutionalised the burgeoning tribal militias in Darfur, in pursuit of a policy of accommodating unsettled Arab groups in productive areas. The Arabs were armed ostensibly so they could defend themselves against the southern Sudanese rebels but in practice they use their guns in their fights with farmers. They also fight among themselves, especially over grazing areas and water holes. Nothing can deter any one tribe, whether farmer or pastoralist, from using its newly acquired firearms to settle old scores with traditional adversaries. The use of firearms has added a new element to the long-standing conflict between nomads and farmers, not only in Sudan but also in other Sahelian countries. The government must find ways of disarming the tribes, or peace will be a long time coming to Darfur.

Civil war

Omar Mohammed, who is himself from the Isaaq clan of northern Somalia, looks at a situation where government intervention went further than supporting one faction in a regional war. In this case the government of Siad Barre, which collapsed early in 1991, was formed from one kinship group and directed its efforts to the promotion of its own interests. Although environmental issues were not the primary causes of the civil war, they are a significant part of the complex of tensions which made possible the escalation of communal rivalry into full-scale war. (see Chapter Two, p30, for an account of the clan system in Somalia.)

War in Somalia
by Omar Mohammed

Territorial intrusions by different clans and subsequent wars have increased as the ecological conditions of Somalia have deteriorated, while modern forms of government have proved ineffective in dealing with the way of life of the Somali nomad.

Before independence, the presence of two different colonial powers, Italy and Britain, in different parts of the country, did not impinge much on the movement, territories or disputes of the different clans, which crossed freely over the boundaries of the European powers in search of pasture and water.

In 1960 northern and southern Somalia gained their independence from Britain and Italy respectively, and united to form the present Somali Republic. The civilian governments of the first nine years of independence regarded nomadism with all its structures and regulations as a fact of Somali socio-economic life. They had no vision of imposing alternative ways and did little, if anything, to change the natural course of things.

Nomads, for their part, hardly saw independence as a change. In

Background: Somalia

In October 1969 the government was overthrown by military coup. Siad Barre took power. In May 1988 war broke out in the north, led by the Somali National Movement (SNM), made up mainly of Isaaqs. SNM attacked Burao and Hargeisa, the capital of the region. The army retaliated with massive bombardment, of civilian as well as rebel military targets. Between January 1989 and September 1990 the government promised, but did not carry out, various reforms: referendum on a new constitution, multi-party elections, liberalisation of the economy, and suspension of anti-human rights laws. By late 1990, war had spread through the country, led by the United Somali Congress (USC) in the centre and the Somali Patriotic Movement (SPM) in the south. In January 1991, power in Mogadishu was seized by the USC.

the words of Ali Hirsi, a 57-year-old Somali nomad who now lives in England as a refugee, they "had neither expectations nor fear of the new, indigenous administrations".

Democratically elected governments succeeded each other. The elections, naturally, reflected the clan system of the country, and "every candidate counted on the votes of his kinsmen", says Ali Hirsi. Politicians were drawn from the small élite class of the time, and their campaigning consisted of persuading their respective clans to back them.

But once the nomads had elected their clansmen candidates, that was almost the end of the story. The successful candidate enjoyed his new privileges and was no longer concerned about his nomadic kinsmen; the nomads saw no way in which he could help or represent their interests (which, in any case, they did not believe could be determined by a government). The governments of these first nine years were governments by the people but not for or to the people, but at least they did not practise repression.

Somali political history changed radically with the assassination in October 1969 of President Abdirashid Sharmarke, the last civilian president of Somalia. Six days after the assassination, Major-General Mohamed Siad Barre took power in a bloodless coup. Immediately, the 1960 constitution of the country was suspended, the National Assembly was dissolved and political parties, which numbered 60 at the time, as well as professional associations were abolished.

President Barre apparently decided quickly to exploit the

structure of the Somali clan system rather than wait to become its victim, and he based his strategy on two main policies: to favour his Daarood clan-family, especially his own Mareehaan clan; and to oppress and undermine the Isaaq, which he saw as the strongest, wealthiest and historically most war-like clan-family. He then juggled with the loyalty of other clans, according to the political situation of the day.

The Daarood clan-family members received special treatment in matters of business and employment, at the expense of other clan-families and especially the Isaaqs who were specifically denied such advantages. In 1990, more than 70% of the top military and civil service posts were held by members of the Daarood clan. Many non-Daarood small businesses went bankrupt as the prices of their goods could not compete with the cheap Daarood goods which were exempted from taxes.

The economic gap between the Daarood and non-Daarood settlements gradually widened as almost all development projects were undertaken in Daarood settlements. One extreme example was the siting of the country's cement plant. One of the world's largest reserves of limestone was discovered in Berbera, a northern Somali

Alan Hutchison/Hutchison Library

The search for water dominates the movement of Somali nomads. Throughout the civil war, and during earlier hostilities, water holes were the first target of attack by one clan on another.

coastal town of the Isaaqs. Yet the authorities decided that the cement plant should be built in a site more than 1,000 km south from Berbera, to which the raw material would have to be transported. In the event, the decision was rejected by the investors and withdrawn.

The 1977 influx of the Ethiopian refugees, as a result of the Somali-Ethiopian war, made matters worse. The refugees, who were predominantly Ogadenis of the Daarood clan-family, were mostly settled in northern, Isaaq, settlements. This was seen by the Isaaqs as a calculated move against them. The government created paramilitary groups among the refugees and recruited others into the national army.

The discontent of the Isaaqs broke out into the open when a group of mostly exiled Isaaqs announced the founding of an opposition group, the Somali National Movement (SNM), in London in 1981. Shortly afterwards, the group sent a mission to Ethiopia, where it established its headquarters. With Ethiopia's backing, the SNM began border operations against the garrisons of the Somali army.

In April 1987, President Barre offered the Ethiopian government a peace treaty in which Somalia gave up its territorial claims on the Ogaden region of Ethiopia in return for depriving the SNM of its Ethiopian bases. When the Ethiopians agreed to the terms, the SNM took a secret decision to attack northern Somalia and establish its base there.

One month after the agreement, the SNM forces captured Burao, strategically the most important town in northern Somalia. By mid-1988, Somalia was involved in one of the worst civil wars Africa has seen, between the government and its supporters on one side and more than five armed but disunited opposition groups on the other.

As a result more than 1 million people have fled to Ethiopia and other parts of the world. Tens of thousands of civilians are also displaced within the country. Hargeisa and four other towns as well as numerous villages and settlements, mostly in the north of the country, have been reduced to rubble. The most conservative estimates put the number of civilians killed in those bombardments or summarily executed in the streets by the government forces at between 50,000 and 60,000.

At the end of 1990, the government introduced a new constitution and legalised opposition parties. Opposition groups commented that the sudden switch to political pluralism was a "futile exercise". By January 1991, the government had collapsed, leaving a fragmented nation and a devastated economy. Ali Mahdi Mohamed of the United Somali Congress was inaugurated president.

Government action

Chadian journalist **Mahamat Hissène** writes about an example in which governments recognised the urgent need to solve a problem of resource allocation. The scene is Lake Chad, which is bordered by Niger, Cameroon, Chad and Nigeria. Demarcating boundaries across or beneath the surface of the lake is not easy but important, as the lake supplies fish, grazing and agricultural lands (on its islands) to an increasing number of people from the four states.

Competition for land is intensifying, and the traditional way of life of the lake people, which pays no attention to legal national boundaries, was creating increasingly frequent problems for the people and for the authorities of the four countries. In 1964, their governments set up the Lake Chad Basin Commission (CBLT) to clarify the borders and to seek and implement solutions. The commission has established an impressive record of containing tension and preventing serious conflict in what could have been an explosive region.

Fluid borders: Lake Chad
by Mahamat Hissène

In the vastness of the lake waters, the birth of an island is monitored very closely, especially by the herders who keep watching out for the appearance of new land on which to graze their oxen. The first group which builds a fairway to reach the island becomes its owner. Others, however, can camp on it to fish, farm or graze the land along with the first-comers.

Apart from belonging to the various states, the islands are also split into clan territories. Friction starts between people of different occupation and becomes exacerbated by differences in nationality. Fortunately, within the framework of the CBLT, the four co-riparian states are completing a border demarcation of the lake.

In his air-conditioned office in N'Djamena, capital of Chad,

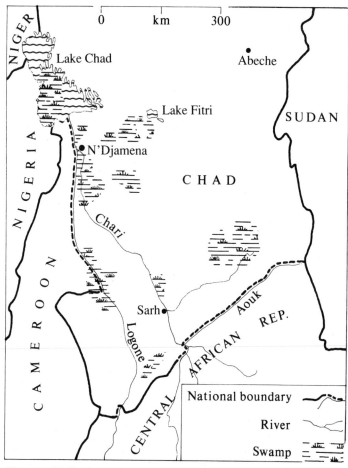

Youssouf MBodou MBami, the incumbent district leader, is trying to be cheerful. "It is true that my district might lose two or three islands, but demarcation is a good thing," he says. MBami is sure that demarcation will not prevent his fellow Boudouma tribesmen and their lakeside neighbours from moving about the waters as in the past; they will, however, have to suppress some ancestral customs if they want to learn to cope with modern national frontiers.

Sarah Errington/Hutchison Library

"The papyrus pirogue reeling in the northern wind."

A bounty of fish

An almost legendary image: the papyrus *pirogue* (canoe) reeling in the northern wind. The shadows of two fishermen, father and son, ripple under the waves.

The Boudouma are fishermen by nature, herders for prestige and, on occasion, farmers. They therefore live on water, from which they draw their income, and keep cattle herds on the islands when they can afford to. Every day when the sun starts to set, they position their lines of hooks or nets. The lake is considered to be one of the richest fishing grounds in the world, although this may no longer be true after the severe 1980 drought. Even today, fishermen, who go out both morning and evening in some seasons, bring back enough fish to feed their families and still have a large surplus to be sold, smoked or dried. Their main outlet is Nigeria, on the western bank, where the fishermen buy manufactured goods. This trade has led to a massive introduction of the Nigerian currency (naira) and of the Hausa language among the Boudouma living in Chad.

If they lived by fishing alone, the Boudouma might not seek to exercise such a peculiar right to the lake islands. In spite of the drop in the quantity of fish and the arrival *en masse* of fishermen of other nationalities, the Boudouma have hardly changed their customs. They are simply more vigilant, largely because of the rising theft of lines and fish. They now have to drop anchor in the open waters of the lake to keep an eye on activities.

Herds of honour

It is for their oxen—the Kouri breed, with their swollen, gourd-like horns—that the Boudouma colonise the islands. Owning a herd of several hundred or even a thousand cattle is the greatest honour for a Boudouma family head. Cattle breeding is for prestige and oxen are only sold as a last resort. Unlike other cattle-breeding groups in the country, the Boudouma do not even have to make a gift of a large number of oxen when they get married. Yet they devote much of their time to their cattle, and family movements on the lake follow the lifecycle of the cattle rather than fishing opportunities. During the high water season, men and oxen go to the mainland in order to avoid the flies and mosquitoes which are rife on the islands, and in the dry season they go into the water to allow their animals to graze the new grass.

The islands are aligned along a north-south axis, the direction of the prevailing winds in this area. Among the Boudouma ethnic group, each clan controls a string of islands, where the families graze their oxen. The animals swim from one island to the next, following fairways cut with machetes between thick papyrus banks. As the water level of the lake drops during the dry season, the various clans keep an eye out for new pastures. As soon as a mound of earth wide enough to accommodate a grazing herd emerges, the clan, which usually occupies other islands along the same line, constructs a fairway to link them with the new island. Thus the land is once again colonised and becomes the property of that clan.

Occasionally, a more remote group colonises an island before its closer neighbours; sometimes, an island may be located between two clan areas. Such events are the main causes of fighting between the clans, even among those of the same district. Arbitration by the customary chief and the administration eventually solves disputes but only after painstaking interpretation of local customs concerning the occupation of the islands. Unfortunately, blood is sometimes shed on the lake's waters.

Growing pressures

The 1970-80 drought drew people to the lake from many different areas. Whilst fishermen from all the co-riparian countries, especially the Nigerians, make most use of the waters, cattle herders (mostly from Chad) and farmers (all nationalities, but mainly Nigerian) have settled down on the fertile new land opened up by

Werner Gartung/Panos Pictures

The rich waters and islands of Lake Chad have long attracted fishermen and farmers from the bordering states. Drought and over-exploitation have gradually depleted resources, increasing tensions between groups— and thus the need to establish clear national boundaries.

the retreating lake waters. The islands now have to support larger populations, with varied and conflicting occupations.

Unlike their neighbours, such as the Kouri and Kanembou, the Boudouma are not keen on farming. Thanks to the richness of the ground, small alluvial plots of land are enough to cover their cereal needs. So, as well as resenting the close mesh of the newcomers' fishing nets, which has been condemned by the Chadian Fisheries and Forestry Department, the Boudouma find that the new settlers' desire to farm the land is incompatible with their livestock breeding. The allocation of space in the islands has been disrupted. Families of all occupations feel restricted and arguments flare up when cattle escape into the fields. And the increasingly numerous farmer-fishermen are beginning to contest the seniority rights of the more mobile herder-fishermen.

Nationality clashes

The mobility of the populations creates complex situations for the administrative authorities. For example, a Nigerian fisherman who goes to Nigeria to sell his fish and comes back to an island with products bought in his country thinks he has done nothing illegal, believing there are no borders on the lake. For the Chadian customs officer, however, such an operation is smuggling, pure and simple. Similar misunderstandings affect fishing, which may be unrestricted in one area and elsewhere subject to regulations and taxes.

In 1976, a tense situation was relieved by the mixed Chadian-Nigerian brigade, whose staff are posted on both sides of the lake. In 1983, more serious incidents put Nigeria and Chad in opposition. Once again, the CBLT restored order. Nevertheless, communities are still increasing on the lake, their numbers swelled by people driven from their homes by drought. Friction is growing. Each community looks for higher support for any claim or grievance, and national pride soon becomes involved.

The "mixed brigade" has been adopted by all member states of the CBLT, and its staff systematically patrol the area. Heads of state organised a gathering of their experts to compare texts on the demarcation of their respective borders. On paper, there is no contradiction, but on site the lake's decrease has caused thousands of new islands to emerge and the land configuration to be greatly altered. The CBLT states have asked a European geographical institute to reset the landmarks and demarcate the boundaries, working with each country's experts.

CHAPTER FIVE
Three Rivers

Of all natural resources, water is the key to life. Throughout the arid lands of the Sahel, it is in short supply, and studies of global warming suggest that the Sahel's major rivers will suffer severe decreases in water flows. Several contributors to this book have described different levels of tension over water—from single families competing with one another to intertribal hostility.

Rivers have the potential to be the cause of conflict on a far larger scale, since many are shared between a number of countries. Different states naturally wish to appropriate the waters on their territory for their own use. Yet action taken upstream—a new dam or changes to flooding and drainage patterns—can dramatically affect agricultural or industrial use of water further down the river. Where a river forms the border between states, action by the people of one country can affect their neighbours on the opposite bank. Cooperation between states is essential if the best use is to be made of this precious resource—and if conflict is to be avoided. This chapter looks at three specific rivers which have been or might be the cause of tension between states: the Beli, the Senegal and the Nile Rivers. Burkinabè **Cheik Kolla Maïga** writes about the first, which has twice been the cause of military action.

Running along the border between Mali and Burkina Faso, the Beli River (190 km long) is a rare source of water in this near-desert region. The river is the centre around which all economic and social activity in the valley revolves. The area is predominantly inhabited by semi-nomadic pastoralist people whose way of life along the river has developed largely without any recognition of national boundaries. Uncertainty about who has rights over land and water has been the source of constant friction between the two countries.

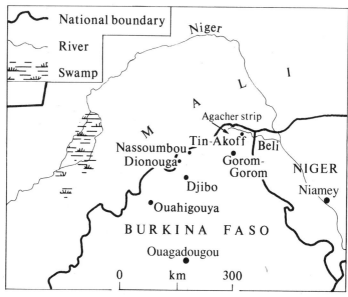

The Beli River valley
by Cheik Kolla Maïga

It is late July, and Mohammed Ag Ahmadi has been in his field since the early hours of the morning. He works steadily, pulling the weeds out of the ground, and casts occasional anxious glances at the clear sky. The last rains were five weeks ago. Will the young millet shoots scattered throughout the field survive until the next rain?

Mohammed Ag Ahmadi is a strong old man. He is a semi-settled Tuareg, and like the other inhabitants of the narrow Agacher strip has been practising agriculture once a year in this border region. Three months earlier he was in Saudi Arabia where, in his own words, he sold his labour on a government building site. When the winter season was over, he returned to his village, Tingassan, which is 9 km from Tin-Akoff, the chief town of Oudalan province in Burkina Faso. His aim was to sow a strip of soil between the village and the Beli River at the first rains, in the hope of harvesting enough to feed his family until the next season...if only the rain would fall more regularly and the grasshoppers would spare the young shoots.

The Agacher strip

The Agacher strip runs alongside the banks of the Beli River in the department of Tin-Akoff in the far north of Burkina Faso, on the border between Burkina and Mali. This strip of fertile land is 160 km long and about 15 km wide. The Beli River, which is 134 km long in Burkina Faso, has its source in neighbouring Mali, and eventually joins the Niger River, flowing eastwards into the Republic of Niger.

Given the scarcity of water and the particular importance of livestock-breeding for the economy of the region, it is not surprising that the Beli River remains the centre around which life revolves, and numerous hamlets inhabited by nomadic populations have built up in the vicinity.

The Agacher strip has been a constant source of dispute between successive Malian and Burkinabè governments. Ever since independence in 1960, Mali claimed ownership of the strip, arguing that the frontier should run up to 15 km south of the river, not to the north as implemented by the Burkinabè.

Travellers to the area are often surprised by what they find. Although an integral part of the near-desert Sahel area, the strip has denser plant cover than people expect. Thorny bushes are scattered throughout the region, with groups of trees thickest around the Beli River and the pools. Tree species include various kinds of acacias (thorn trees), bohemias and jujube (*Zizyphus jujuba*) trees, which adapt well to the ubiquitous sand and degraded flinty soils. This tenacious and surprising plant cover is worth protecting, come what may, against the many threats, not least of which are goats and sheep. It may be sparse, but the vegetation creates an effective natural defence against the plague of sand dunes which are spreading rapidly from the western side of the strip.

There are around 12,000 people living in the 14 villages of the Tin-Akoff department, the vast majority of them Muslim. The main characteristic of the populations in the department, and apparently in the whole border area, is a sense of unity overriding ethnic difference. For example, although the people belong to three different ethnic groups, Tuareg, Bella, and Fulani, the use of the Tamashek (Tuareg) language is widespread. In some villages the Wara-wara Fulani do not remember their original language of Fulfulde, and Tamashek has become their mother-tongue.

On either side of the border live families who were separated arbitrarily by the frontier. We met some Tuareg who claimed that not long ago they were Malians and today are Burkinabè while another part of their family remains in Mali.

Despite the region's domination by the river, lack of control over the water supply is the main constraint on economic activities. Some pools quite far from the river bed are supplied by the Beli streams, but the main water course is unharnessed and flows into the Niger River. During the short rainy season, thunderstorms flood the area, cutting it off from the rest of the country and making the few rough tracks impassable. After the rainy season the rapidity of the flow washes away soil, while for most of the rest of the year, there are serious difficulties with supplies.

Because of this variability of rainfall and the fact that irrigation has not been developed, agricultural activities are poor. The main economic and culturally valued activity remains herding, of camels, oxen, sheep and goats. The social and economic importance of livestock gives rise to an almost obsessive attachment to animals—raising livestock assumes almost mystical significance. Throughout this area, animals are spared from working. In popular love-songs, women's beauty is often symbolised by the cow and to tell someone she is "as beautiful as a cow" is a real compliment.

Potential causes of conflict: ownership

Not surprisingly, satisfying the herds' needs for water and fodder occupies much of the people's energy. Their continual wandering in search of pasture and water frequently leads them to cross the frontier, which has always been irrelevant to these nomadic populations.

In the hottest months, from March to June, the Beli River dries up completely, and the herders are forced to move their animals to other water points. According to one inhabitant of Wassa-Kose, 14 km from Tin-Akoff, some shepherds keep their women and children away from the wells to ensure their thirsty animals get enough water.

For the rest of the dry season, which lasts for eight or nine months, the river is the main source of water, and an exodus takes place from the borderlands and surrounding areas to the river. This movement of herds from frontier villages does not in itself cause any difficulties. The problems that arise concern who has rights over the resources close to the river.

For the periods when the Sahel's rivers no longer flow, scattered pools are the only source of water.

"We and the people from Mali who bring their herds here, we are one and the same. There is no conflict between us," confided Mohammed Ag Ahmadi in the Burkinabè village of Tingassan. "What has irritated us is the way our neighbours pretend that the Beli is exclusively theirs to make use of. The water which flows here is a gift of God and nobody has the right to bar access to it. Since the time of my parents, it has always been this way. But our brothers from Mali pretend that the Beli is part of their country and this we cannot accept. They must understand that the Beli is part of Burkina and then there will be no further problems between us."

Most people view the border as a rather bizarre phenomenon, and many go regularly to Bakali in Mali or other frontier villages in search of pasture. This area is rich in fonio (*Digitaria exilis*), a wild grass producing an edible grain. Its harvest attracts people from both sides of the border, since the crop provides a livelihood for the people, and the stubble provides grazing during the long dry season. "There's no problem with this," everyone assured us, although a young man at Wassa-Kose said that he had heard that the chiefs of the villages in Mali were exacting tribute for the use of their pasture land. If this is true, it could be a potential source of conflict.

After the drought

The grazing of livestock can damage the shrubs growing in the sandy soil. The herds leave little in their path and certain shrubs are unable to regenerate because of the regular passage of livestock.

Naturally, the people in nearby villages resent this and rarely miss an opportunity to say so. Only occasionally does this go beyond registering a complaint. But various initiatives by agricultural officials charged with protecting vegetation from migrating livestock have resulted in small conflicts.

Animal theft is the crucial problem in the region. The great drought of 1968-73 decimated much of the livestock on both sides of the border. Many herders were ruined, or sought other means of making a living. Whatever the cost, it was vital to restore their herds and flocks, around which revolve marriage, festivals and other social events. And according to many people interviewed, in this period armed Malians showed no hesitation in invading villages in Upper Volta (as Burkina Faso was then known) to steal herds of cattle and camels. This cattle raiding, they say, was at the root of the conflict in 1974.

The phenomenon continues today. Armed bands from Mali cross the border into Burkina and take away herds, firing shots in the air to dissuade anyone trying to stop them. Because of this, owning a gun is considered a necessity by people throughout the Agacher strip. The prefect of Tin-Akoff confirmed this, displaying numerous applications for the possession of firearms. "We must arm ourselves in order to face these livestock thieves," Ag Ahmadi assured us, "for it's the only measure which frightens them." In virtually all the villages visited there were men carrying guns. "How do you get them?" we asked. "In Mali, in exchange for a camel, you can get a good gun," Ag Ahmadi confided. "So we don't hesitate—because guns allow us to protect our riches."

The Burkinabè state is attempting to control this influx of weapons, but the atmosphere of insecurity is such that people still wish to carry arms.

Conflict

By 1973, an international disaster had been declared in the Sahel. The Food and Agriculture Organisation (FAO) estimated that 25% of the region's cattle and sheep had died. Cattle losses were estimated at 20-40% in Mali and 10-20% in Upper Volta. These figures do not include the deliberate slaughtering of animals, by herders who realised that their stock would not survive the dry season. In some areas, stock loss was 100% [1].

CILSS estimated that between 50,000 and 100,000 people died

in the six francophone countries of the Sahel as a result of the drought.

The rains returned in June 1974. As soon as the first drops fell, farmers took up their hoes. By July, the Beli River was full again, providing drinking water and turning the surrounding land into a valuable marshy grazing area. October saw the first real harvest in the area for seven years.

Drought had made the Beli water seem even more valuable. A meeting was held between the authorities of Mali and Upper Volta in September 1974, and the Voltaics declared that they had a right to deny Malian herders access to water supplies in the disputed Agacher strip. (Normal practice would have been to allow free access, even if it were accepted that the territory did belong to Upper Volta.)

The response was swift and unprecedented. In December 1974, Malian troops and tanks moved in to occupy part of the disputed area. Within days, the opposing forces clashed, resulting in at least one death and several casualties. The encounter left Malian troops controlling much of the disputed area.

Appeals from neighbouring countries and from the Organisation of African Unity (OAU) resulted in agreement on the principle of mediation, and a commission was established. Fighting broke out again six months later but, again with persuasion from neighbouring governments, the governments of Mali and Upper Volta signed an agreement for a mediation commission. The Agacher strip was lightly administered by Mali from then on.

Meanwhile drought had returned to the region. In 1982, the July rains arrived early on both sides of the border. Seeds germinated, but then shrivelled in the scorching sun. The rainy season failed again in 1983, and the October harvest was ruined in most Sahelian countries. In the north of Upper Volta, as wells were reduced to a trickle and fodder shortages increased, people were forced to sell their cattle for less than one sixth of the normal price. The river seemed worthless, and both countries agreed to submit the border dispute for arbitration at the International Court of Justice in The Hague.

Better rainfall returned to some parts of the Sahel in 1984, and improved significantly in 1985. Dried-out riverbeds flowed with water again, and withered pastures became lush.

In December 1985, in a startling repeat of the pattern set by the conflict 11 years earlier, Mali launched an extensive military attack against Burkina Faso. Mali argued that the presence, since mid-December, of Burkinabè officials who were conducting a census in the disputed strip of land, amounted to attempted annexation of the territory. They also claimed that Malian officials had been mistreated by soldiers accompanying the census officials.

A Malian battalion of Soviet-built tanks attacked Burkinabè ground troops at Dionouga. Mali also launched air attacks against the Burkinabè towns of Ouahigouya, Djibo and Nassoumbou, despite the fact that these are all outside the disputed area. It followed these with an airstrike on Koloko, some 300 km away from the strip, and near to Burkina's second largest town, Bobo Dioulasso. Burkina retaliated with an air attack on the southern Malian town of Sikasso, surprising many observers who had not known that impoverished Burkina Faso possessed any combat aircraft at all.

After five days, a ceasefire was signed by both countries, negotiated under the auspices of Senegal's President Abdou Diouf, then OAU chairman. Estimates of the number of casualties varied from 40 to 300. A large number of people living in the Agacher strip were caught up in the fighting and rendered destitute, losing animals and grain to the soldiers.

In January 1986, the two heads of state, President Traoré of Mali, and President Sankara of Burkina, met in Côte d'Ivoire, shook hands and embraced. They agreed that the situation regarding the disputed territory should return to what it had been before the conflict, pending the results of international arbitration; in effect, the area would be mostly administered by Mali. The International Court of Justice delivered its judgement in December 1986, defining the frontier in terms of the scarce natural resources. It ruled that pools should be divided "in an equitable manner", and that the frontier should run along the river itself. The judgement was accepted by both governments [2].

The future

The Beli is the only significant source of water in the zone. By custom and tradition, the Burkinabè people draw little profit from it. "The Beli is full of fish, but unfortunately my people are little interested in this," explained the prefect of Tin-Akoff. So Nigerien and Malian fishermen catch the fish, which they then sell back to the local population. Fish has not become an essential part of the diet of the Bella, Fulani and Tuareg, who are convinced that nothing is as good as their millet cakes with butter and milk.

Nevertheless, owing to a shortage of staple foods and following the advice of health officials, there is an increasing market for the fishermen's catch. For the time being, the local people are content to buy fish instead of catching it themselves. A Bella man, when asked the reason why, replied that he was not so stupid as to undo his turban so that women might see his naked head, just for the sake of some fish!

As well as fishing potential, there are opportunities for market gardening all along the Beli. At the moment, only a few officials in Tin-Akoff have entered the business, and they are having great success with carrots, cabbages, aubergines and potatoes. The indigenous people do not take this activity seriously partly, it seems, because of their dietary habits, and also perhaps from uncertainty about marketing the produce.

Finally, gold deposits are being found throughout the sub-region, drawing people from both sides of the border. The main site at Essakane, near the border with Niger, has attracted many people from Mali, Niger, Ghana, Nigeria and elsewhere. In spite of the presence of law-enforcement authorities, however, there are often fights and thefts. Prostitutes have followed the prospectors. Living and working conditions are deplorable and diseases are rife.

Overall, there are many economic activities that could be promoted in order to diversify the food supply and to create income for the young people who now leave the region in search of work. Each year, after the harvest, they depart in droves to neighbouring Côte d'Ivoire. The money they earn enables them to buy clothes and radios; anything left over is spent on millet and livestock. Back home, the young people show off their new possessions. This often causes trouble, as many village women have eyes only for the smartly dressed boys who have returned from abroad.

The departure of so many young people—and some older men such as Mohammed Ag Ahmadi, who prefer to go to Saudi Arabia to sell their labour—results in a considerable inflow of money, almost all of which is invested in livestock. Throughout the whole department, only one merchant in Tin-Akoff has a savings account at the Gorom-Gorom station, the main centre in the province.

The Senegal River valley

> We pinned all our hopes on the building of the dams along the river. For the local people, however, the scheme has caused a large number of problems....The government has tried to take the land... so that they can manage it themselves. But they have had to face opposition, since the land is so much part of the people that they will not give it up easily to strangers.
> *Ahmedou Ba, diplomat, Mauritania*

Mauritanian **Boubakar Ba** looks at a situation where there has been no formal military invasion by one country of another but where the impact of hostilities on the countries concerned, Senegal and Mauritania, has probably been more widespread and longer-term. Tension over the Senegal River's resources has coincided with a number of other longstanding problems, to do with environmental degradation, diminution of resources and ethnic difficulties.

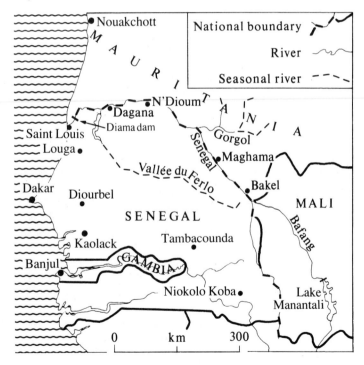

Boubakar Ba argues that, although they started quite suddenly, the hostilities have roots in many years of neglect by the Mauritanian government of crucial questions over the allocation of the country's resources, and in the consequent intense agricultural and demographic pressure on the river and its fertile banks.

Uneven development in Mauritania
by Boubakar Ba

Stories, legends and anecdotes concerning drought and the search for water remain alive in the Sahelian collective consciousness. One such legend is that of the parakeet bearing a millet stalk which led the Fulbe, ancestors of the Haal Pulaar'en, to the Senegal River. According to the Wagadu legend of the Soninke, not a single drop of water fell for seven years, seven months and seven days until salvation came from a magic drum which summoned the rain.

Nowadays, the bulk of the Mauritanian population and the country's economic activities are concentrated in the Senegal River basin and along the seaboard, in less than a quarter of the national territory. While natural conditions have undoubtedly played a large part in bringing about this situation, politicians and Mauritanian society as a whole also bear a heavy responsibility for the way land and natural resources are allocated.

Even today, Mauritanians in general, including top-level officials, do not include protecting or improving the habitat in their vision of the country's future. Those responsible for development say: "We do not have the means to conduct a balanced overall policy for the development of our territory; we have to bow to our donors' demands." This is a facile argument which does not explain why things were just the same before colonisation, or why attempts to control pollution and improve the environment are so derisory.

Mauritania is the most Saharan of the Sahelian countries. It should have a first-class ministerial department making sure that ecological factors are taken into account in all projects, in every aspect of the country's economic and social life, and in the training of future generations. As it is, environmental matters are covered by a section of the Ministry of Rural Development. It is not surprising that many projects simply ignore such concerns.

Mauritania's European and North American partners justify concentrating their agricultural investments in the Senegal River

Background: the Senegal River

For centuries, farming people have settled along both sides of the Senegal River, which forms the border between Senegal to the south and Mauritania to the north, using the river's annual floods to assist their cultivation. Many communities straddled both sides of the river and people passed regularly from one bank to the other. For decades the governments of the region, first colonial then national, dreamt of harnessing the river's resources for industrial development. These plans finally came to fruition in the 1970s with the establishment of the Organisation for the Exploitation of the Senegal River (OMVS), which brought the governments of Mali, Mauritania and Senegal into close cooperation.

Although there was local opposition to the developments, the governments collaborated effectively. Two dams were built in the 1980s, and irrigated areas for rice-growing were established along both sides of the river. Doubts began to emerge about the debts incurred and the cost-effectiveness of the rice-growing scheme. But there was no interstate hostility until April 1989, when violence erupted between Senegal and Mauritania, affecting thousands of people in both countries. The tension between the two states continues today.

basin by saying that it is where the people, the land and the water are. This is inaccurate, since southeast Mauritania also has "people, land and water" but is neglected by foreign donors. It would be possible to carry out agro-pastoral projects there which could encourage a better distribution of population, and relieve the overcrowded areas which are threatened with ecological disaster. The attitude of the international partners stems largely from a concern for the profitability of investments, and from the absence of a balanced approach to territorial development by the government.

Consequences of neglect

The situation in Tagant region, central Mauritania, is typical of the serious consequences of this policy of neglecting the desert and semi-desert areas of the country. Tidjikja and the surrounding region are still famous for the quality of their dates, which play an important part in the traditional diet of the nomads. However, Tagant dates have become a luxury for the average Mauritanian; and only the most well-off can afford them today.

Over the last 20 years, water has become scarce and the water table is falling dangerously low. Previously, the run-off from the *batha* (rainwater streams from the mountains) replenished underground water supplies. Wells used to be no more than 10 metres deep in the palm-groves. Nowadays, the owners of the palm-groves have to dig deeper. Since they hit solid rock at 15 metres, they have to use dynamite, which is expensive. The growing cycle of the Tagant palm trees is severely disrupted by the lack of water.

The persistence of drought, the disappearance of vegetation and the erosion of the soil have worsened another problem: the sanding-up of the palm-groves. According to the most optimistic estimates, at least 60% of the palm-groves, which once contained about 100,000 trees, have been submerged by sand before the eyes of their despairing owners. Neither the state nor its northern partners have made any attempt to halt the process, let alone reverse it. The torrential rains of 1988 and 1989 did not help the sanding-up, although they did replenish the water-table and make the countryside green again.

The Senegal River valley development

After a decade of drought in the 1970s, which had badly affected Mauritania and its people, thousands of nomadic herders were pushing southwards. At certain times of the year water points in the north always dry up, and grazing becomes scarce. Herders who used to cross the borders into Mali and Senegal crowded into the more humid south and southeast parts of Mauritania. The completion of the Diama and Manantali dams by OMVS in the 1980s brought impoverished people from the Mauritanian countryside flocking to the valley to claim a small plot of land. The dams gave rise to great hopes of an end to the years of want, and competition for land there became fierce.

The valley's human and animal carrying capacity is being greatly exceeded. The alarm bells are not yet ringing, even though 10 years ago environmental degradation in the valley first became evident, both to the people living alongside the river and to those in the Senegalese and Mauritanian hinterlands. Sandstorms became more frequent and severe, their effects being felt as far away as Senegal's capital, Dakar.

Indiscriminate wood-cutting, uncontrolled exploitation of

underground water, the disappearance of vegetation and soil degradation are all hastening the destruction of the area's life-support systems. Where forests used to obscure the horizon, it is now possible to glimpse the minarets of mosques in villages a dozen kilometres away. Many trees died in the drought, and with the complicity of the forest guards, charcoal producers devastated the bulk of the remaining classified forests.

Fauna and flora are gradually disappearing: in Nouakchott, the Mauritanian capital, children now recognise certain animals only in books and films, whereas 20 years ago deer, guinea-fowl and bustards were a common sight.

The first victims of these threats to the environment are, above all, women and young people. A popular saying here is that "land is a father who does not recognise his daughters". Indeed, women are precluded from inheriting land, despite the long-standing Muslim influence. They, along with the young people, are the last to be given access to a plot in the family landholdings, especially on the coveted *waalo* lands: the alluvial plains which are flooded regularly by the river. Pressure on land is increasing, and it is clear that the position of women is getting worse. Village women, who bear the daily burden of cooking and fetching water and firewood, are having to travel further and further to find dead wood.

Conflict in the valley

Competition for resources often takes the form of rivalry between ethnic groups. This is just the continuation of a trend begun generations ago. Faced with adverse natural conditions to which they were unable to find long-term solutions, social groups of different ethnic origins have for centuries conflicted or cooperated over the control of the land in the Senegal River valley.

There are four ethnic groups living in Mauritania: Arabs, and three groups of black Africans: Haal Pulaar'en, Soninke and Wolof. The Arabs include the Haratines, as well as the "white Moors". The black African origin of the Haratines is beyond doubt, yet their language, culture and identity are Arab (because they were for centuries enslaved to white masters). The "white Moors" are descended from both the Berber Arabs and black African groups from the Sahara and this is why so many shades of skin colour are to be found among them. The Haal Pulaar'en are no less mixed, ethnically and culturally. Their oral traditions link them to the

Fulbe, Soninke and Mandinka empires. In historical terms, Arab-Berber, Wolof and Serer influence is evident.

Intermarrying extensively and drawing mutual enrichment from their differences, all these people have over the centuries forged their identity as Mauritanians.

But the competition for land in the Senegal River valley, exacerbated by drought and the OMVS development, has injected a hostility into relations between ethnic groups. The local population in the upper and middle reaches of the Senegal River valley are generally black Africans, whereas the people coming down from the north are mainly Arabs. After Mauritania became independent in 1960, the age-old struggles to control the land became part of the competition for political power between these two broad ethnic groups. This focused initially on the constitution of the post-colonial administration and, from the mid-1960s, on education and training, particularly on the place of the Arabic language in the Mauritanian education system.

With the filling up of the reservoirs behind the dams, and without any policies in favour of balanced territorial development, intercommunal competition for political and economic power is now also focused on control of the valley and its development.

The Senegal River valley is also the theatre for profound agrarian upheavals, because of the OMVS dams. Many sectors of society are competing strongly to stamp their vision of the world on the economy: capitalism, the old tenant arrangements (usually tied up with feudalism), and the new democratic movement based on small-scale production and voluntary peasant cooperation.

It is quite clear that an inappropriate approach to the environment and to land use is one reason for the exacerbation of agrarian conflicts in this area. But the specifically ethnic nature of the disputes over land-holdings in the Senegal River valley is mainly the result of the apparent ambition of the Mauritanian state to modify the balance between communities, to the advantage of the Arabs and to the detriment of the black Africans. Even though some international organisations, such as the World Bank, may marvel at the undeniably positive results achieved by Mauritanian private citizens in the Senegal River basin, they often forget that the basis of these successes is precarious and unsustainable, since it stems from the domination of a single group—the Arabs—over the others.

The events of 1989

Intensifying competition for living space has greatly aggravated relations between Mauritania and Senegal. The events of April-May 1989 took place within a context of general social and economic crisis in the two countries. Competition for daily survival was, and remains, extremely fierce. The most disadvantaged tended to blame all their ills on the "others", the "foreigners". Xenophobia was rampant. This is a major reason why the incidents were so extensive and took such a deadly turn.

The river valley had traditionally been farmed by black Africans of both Senegalese and Mauritanian nationality. Some villages on the Senegalese side of the border had been populated by black Africans of Mauritanian origin, while generations of Senegalese farmers had cultivated fields on the Mauritanian side of the border.

In April 1989, two Senegalese villagers were killed on the island of Doundou Khore, in a dispute over grazing rights. Mauritanian border guards kidnapped another 13 Senegalese villagers. The killings created an immediate furore in the nearby Senegalese town of Bakel but the real violence began two weeks later.

In Senegal, it started with the looting of Mauritanian shops by large crowds of people in Dakar, and in its suburbs, Pikine and

A dispute over grazing rights flared up into large-scale riots in Senegal and Mauritania in 1989— around 260 people died.

Thiaroye. Many Mauritanians were beaten up. Immediately, retaliatory attacks were launched against Senegalese in Mauritania, mainly in the Sebkha and El Mina poor quarters of Nouakchott. A number of Senegalese were killed.

From then on, the violence escalated on both sides. Around 200 people were killed in Mauritania and between 50 and 60 in Senegal. Thousands were forced to take refuge in official or religious buildings, having lost everything they had acquired through years of hard work in the country many considered their own.

Some 300,000 Mauritanians had been living in Senegal, and 30,000-40,000 Senegalese in Mauritania. In Senegal, 85% of the petty commerce sector in Senegal was Mauritanian-owned. Local Mauritanian shopkeepers were often also bankers, money-lenders and friends to many Senegalese. In Mauritania, too, a large number of Senegalese were a vital skilled link in the economic chain: plumbers, carpenters, mechanics and electricians.

As a result of the killings, up to 200,000 penniless Mauritanians flooded back from Senegal.

"Deportees"

But in Mauritania another tragedy emerged alongside these events. Thousands of black Mauritanians were rounded up in their villages, stripped of their possessions and identity cards and shipped across the river to the Senegalese bank. They gathered in scattered camps along the tarmac road that skirts Senegal's northern border. The Senegalese authorities said that Mauritania had expelled this group of its own citizens because of a racist policy of "denegrification".

The media and international opinion regard them as "deportees", as the vast majority have been expelled from their country by the Mauritanian authorities themselves. More than 90% of them are Fulbe agro-pastoralists and nomadic herders. The Senegalese deplore the fact that these nomads should have been expelled from their own country. They are not involved in the struggle for power in Mauritania, which is largely among those who are sedentary and especially those who have received further education. So why should Fulbe herders be the victims of expulsion decreed by the Mauritanian authorities?

The administration and the forces of law and order, who covet their livestock, made the Fulbe their target during the moments of madness which shook Mauritania and Senegal in April and May

1989 and which continue to bring grief to black Mauritanians.

Relations between the two countries continued to deteriorate during the summer of 1989, resulting in a complete rupture of diplomatic, trade and transport links, a vitriolic press war in both countries, and occasional shelling and small-arms fire across the river. Both countries demanded appropriate levels of compensation.

Mauritanian refugees in Senegal

The Senegal bank of the river was suffering some of the same problems as the Mauritanian side: increasing population and pressure on resources. The massive influx of Mauritanian deportees in May 1989 could not fail to aggravate an already worrying situation. This was due not only to the large numbers flooding in but also to their concentration in a small area. The carrying capacity of the Senegalese bank of the river was severely strained. People seem to be taking a long time to wake up to the need to protect the valley from the increasing environmental pressures.

The main road from Saint Louis to Bakel became the focus of the refugee settlements. In order to build their huts, the refugees had to cut a massive amount of wood and gather large quantities of straw. As they poured in, supplies of these resources became scarcer. In Bokki Diawé and Orkodjéré, for example, the last arrivals were unable to build huts of wood and straw and, despite the torrid heat, had to shelter by day under steaming canvas.

At N'Dioum, in order to build the school classrooms, the refugees had to resort to the United Nations High Commission for Refugees (UNHCR) to get the necessary wood for the frame. In the Thiabe camp just outside the town of Dagana, the deportees had to travel about 20 km to obtain a load of wood.

The case of Mamadou Diawo is typical. A former manager in a Mauritanian public sector company, he has become a wood-seller in Dagana. Every morning, after 6 o'clock prayers, he sets off for the wood-cutting area, arriving at about 9 o'clock. By around 11 o'clock, his two donkeys are heavily laden. He returns to camp to make up the small piles of wood which the refugees and town-dwellers come to buy. His household eats better than most in the camp.

The camps of Mauritanian refugees stretch over several hundred kilometres from Dagana to Bakel, everywhere showing the same picture of wretched huts and ragged children. How many refugees

The continued presence of refugees, like these Mauritanians in Senegal, can add to the pressures on an already overstretched environment.

are there? Some say 50,000, others claim 100,000. A figure of 70,000 is quoted by the Association of Mauritanian Refugees in Senegal (ARMS). Some idea of their situation can be grasped by the following descriptions of two camps.

N'Dioum camp

When the 2,212 deportees arrived at N'Dioum, conditions were particularly appalling, despite the fraternal welcome offered by the local people. As the new arrivals were destitute, they were exposed to the worst of a particularly rainy season. With the help of UNHCR and some non-governmental organisations (NGOs), conditions were improved and supplies organised more effectively. A local committee now supervises camp life. Running water has been supplied and serious health problems are dealt with at a nearby hospital, while minor ailments are treated at a camp health post.

Political activity is lively. As a result of the collective trauma of 1989, most people now reject the once prevailing intolerance. A consensus is being forged as to the need for all refugees to work together, to improve their living conditions and to persevere in exploring all possible ways of returning to Mauritania and to set up democratic relationships between the different ethnic groups.

As they become more and more convinced of the need for self-reliance, the refugees in N'Dioum have decided to take over the production of certain foodstuffs, organise the education of their children and give adult literacy classes.

Several projects have been started: one of these, a market garden set up by the women in the camp, is of particular interest. Originally planned for the men, this garden was taken over, despite some opposition, by the women, who were formerly restricted to domestic work and childcare and excluded from political, trade union and economic activities in the camp.

Orkodjéré camp

Some 300 km to the east of N'Dioum is Orkodjéré camp, in Matam department. It contains 2,500 individuals, mainly nomadic herders. The remainder are sedentary farmers and former migrant workers who have returned from France, Gabon and Côte d'Ivoire.

On arrival, the refugees were welcomed with spontaneous generosity by the local population, especially the young people. With the help of the Federation of Fouta Development Associations (FAFD) and the NGO Médecins sans Frontières, the accommodation areas were renovated and latrines constructed. Orkodjéré enjoys better living conditions than any other refugee camp in Senegal. Since April 1990, a local ARMS committee has been dealing with the collective concerns and activities of the refugees.

Initially, the refugees harboured many illusions about a rapid settlement of the conflict, and foresaw an immediate return to their country of origin. For this reason, they behaved passively, and were completely dependent on international assistance for their survival. As time went on, their attitude became much more positive. They designed and implemented numerous projects producing goods necessary for their subsistence, education and health.

As in N'Dioum, market gardening is the province of the women, who have organised themselves into cooperatives. One of these has 535 members, of whom 274 are involved in productive concerns. The first experiments gave good results and dry-season production is under way. Encouraged by their success, the women are planning to widen their activities to include sewing, dyeing and the marketing of milk.

Strained relationships

As a result of the demographic pressure exerted on the south bank of the Senegal River by the influx of refugees, areas of conflict are developing in their relationship with their Senegalese hosts.

The Senegalese returnees (those who formerly lived in Mauritania as migrant workers) think, for example, that it is the presence of these Mauritanian deportees in their country which is depriving them of UNHCR food rations. In order to improve their daily diet by including some meat or fish, the refugees sell some of the goods given to them by the UNHCR. In N'Dioum refugee camp this practice has caused the price of a kilo of millet to fall, provoking the anger of local producers. At many water points, the refugees and their hosts often compete with each other for domestic supplies or to water their livestock.

The future

People throughout history have felt a deep attachment to the land of their forebears. Here more than elsewhere, this attachment is accompanied by an almost unmatchable emotionalism. This is why the battle to gain control over the land has claimed hundreds of victims, and will claim many more.

The repercussions of the violence will be felt in both countries for many years to come. At the height of the war of words in the summer of 1989, following the fighting, Senegal announced that the border between the two countries really lies north of the river, and not along the middle, in the way that had been accepted so far. They said that the latter arrangement had been made by former Presidents Senghor of Senegal and Heydallah of Mauritania to facilitate the OMVS development, but that Senegal would now insist on applying a 1933 French colonial decree which fixed the border along the northernmost bank of the floodplain of the river.

Since almost all the agriculture in the river valley is floodplain agriculture, the strict application of this decree would mean Senegal gaining hundreds of thousands of hectares of fertile land hitherto considered Mauritanian. In September 1989 the two states agreed to restore diplomatic relations, despite wide differences over key issues. Ever since the OMVS scheme started, control of the river became a practical possibility, as did food self-sufficiency in Mali, Senegal and Mauritania. But now the conflict raises major questions about the long-term workability of such multi-state schemes. These questions are directly relevant to the debate about future shared management of the waters of the Nile.

The River Nile

Conflicts over the use of the Nile have caused tensions for centuries, and demonstrate the dangers of nation states trying to exercise exclusive sovereignty over a shared resource such as water.

The Nile: lifeblood or bloodshed?

The River Nile is the source of some of Africa's most complex problems of water allocation. The Nile basin touches 10 states: Egypt, Sudan, Central African Republic, Zaire, Uganda, Rwanda, Burundi, Tanzania, Kenya and Ethiopia. The White Nile has its origins in the central African lakes, and is the only drainage outlet from Lake Victoria, at Jinja in Uganda. The Blue Nile drains Lake Tana in the Ethiopian highlands and supplies around 70% of the water in the Nile. The White and the Blue Niles join at Khartoum in Sudan.

The Nile is the longest river in the world, some 6,842 km, ending in the Mediterranean. But it is nonetheless small in volume, very much less than the Amazon or the Congo. Much of this is explained by huge seasonal variations, with 80% of all the water that flows downstream to Egypt coming in just three months.The Nile water is important to all the countries it flows through. But it is the lifeblood of Egypt, a country which is 96% desert. And Egypt is at the end of the line, vulnerable to the actions of the upstream states.

Egypt once produced much of the grain needed for the Roman Empire, although Cairo gets just 30 mm of rain a year. In 1800, the population of Egypt was 4 million; today it is 50 million, growing at 3% per year and still surviving off the same river. The former British prime minister, Winston Churchill, compared Egypt to "a deep-sea diver whose air is provided by the long and well-known tube of the Nile".

The British used the Nile as a weapon against Egyptian nationalism throughout their colonial rule in Sudan. But recognising Egypt's dependence on the river, a number of agreements were imposed during British colonial times that prohibited any

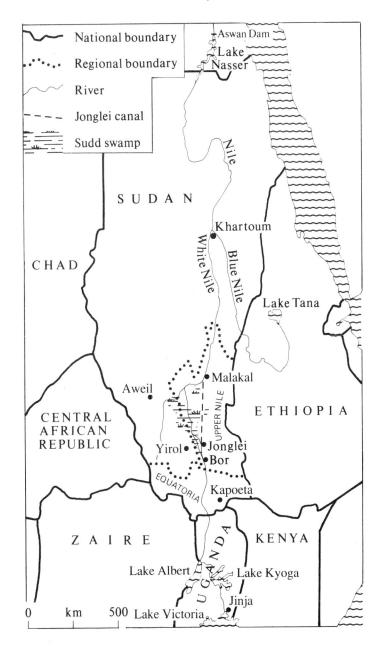

National boundary
Regional boundary
River
Jonglei canal
Sudd swamp

Aswan Dam
Lake Nasser
Nile
SUDAN
Khartoum
CHAD
White Nile
Blue Nile
Lake Tana
Malakal
Aweil
UPPER NILE
ETHIOPIA
CENTRAL
AFRICAN
REPUBLIC
Yirol
Jonglei
Bor
EQUATORIA
Kapoeta
ZAIRE
UGANDA
KENYA
Lake Albert
Lake Kyoga
0   km   500   Lake Victoria
Jinja

construction which would obstruct the flow of the main river.

The 1929 Nile Waters Agreement between Egypt and Britain stated: "It is realised that the development of the Sudan requires a quantity of water greater than that which has so far been utilised" and agreed to "such an increase of this quantity as does not infringe Egypt's natural and historical rights in the waters of the Nile and its requirements of agricultural extension". It added that no measures were to be taken which "would reduce the quantity of water arriving in Egypt, or modify the date of its arrival, or lower its level".

Thirty years later, in 1959, a bilateral agreement between Egypt and Sudan allowed Egypt to construct the Aswan dam. The Aswan dam holds back a volume equivalent to two years of Nile flow, thus successfully regulating the main source of Egypt's economy largely within its own national borders.

Regional war?

With the exception of the 1959 agreement between Sudan and Egypt, no agreement on the uses of the Nile has been reached since Sudan's independence in 1956. The United Nations Development Programme (UNDP) raised the issue in 1985, and again at a meeting in Niamey in 1988 of the UN Economic Commission for Africa. Egypt, Sudan and Ethiopia all intend to expand their irrigated agriculture, to feed their growing populations.

Upstream, Ethiopia has plans to use more water from the Blue Nile, which would directly affect Egypt's water supplies. Ethiopia's main strategic asset is water. Almost 50 sites have been identified for hydro-electric power in the Nile basin area of Ethiopia, and plans have been published for irrigated agriculture which would take 60 million cubic metres of water. It seems that only lack of funds and continuing conflict are preventing Ethiopia's plan to use irrigation to support 0.5 million resettled peasants from the degraded highlands (see Chapter Seven, p122). However, in January 1990 Ethiopia's Minister of Foreign Affairs visited Cairo and firmly denied rumours that his government was about to construct dams, with Israeli help. Despite this denial, the Sudanese government magazine *Sudanow* carried a report six months later that "Israel plans to establish dams on the Blue Nile in Ethiopia, which would mean less water left for both Sudan and Egypt [3]."

In 1990, it was reported that Egyptian scientists had obtained spectacular results from test-drilling for underground water reserves in the Western Desert. "There seems to be a great deal more ground water than we had thought possible for the whole continent," according to Dr Farouk El-Baz [4]. But while these reserves may lessen Egypt's own dependence on the Nile, they do not reduce the need for regional agreement on water use. This need is heightened by studies suggesting that the Nile waters may reduce rapidly as a result of global warming, thus heightening the risk of conflict over diminishing natural resources.

At the United Nations water conference in Argentina in 1977, Ethiopia stressed "the sovereign right of any riparian state, in the absence of an international agreement, to proceed unilaterally with the development of water resources within its territory". Then-President Anwar Sadat of Egypt replied the following year: "We depend upon the Nile one hundred per cent. We shall never hesitate [to act], because it is a matter of life and death."

In 1985, Egypt's Minister of State for Foreign Affairs, Dr Boutros-Ghali, warned that "the next war in our region will be over the waters of the Nile, not politics". Colonel Muammar Gaddafi agrees. He told the General People's Congress in Tripoli in March 1990: "The struggle taking place now in the Horn of Africa and in southern Sudan is over the control of the sources of the Nile....Any encroachment on the waters of the Nile basin will have an extreme effect on Egypt in the future. This is the fact behind the American and Israeli drive for a presence south of Egypt."

Liba Taylor/Hutchison Library

"The next war in our region will be over the waters of the Nile, not politics."

The southern Sudanese journalist **Nhial Bol Aken** writes about how use of the Nile waters has been a major cause of north-south conflict in Sudan.

Civil war in Sudan
by Nhial Bol Aken

The 1959 agreement between Egypt and Sudan, which enabled Egypt to build the Aswan dam, also stipulated that Sudan would build a 300 km canal from the village of Jonglei to Malakal, with costs to be shared between Egypt and Sudan.

The idea for the Jonglei canal was first conceived by the British in 1894. Fifty-five billion cubic metres of water are lost each year in southern Sudan, through evaporation and seepage in the Sudd, one of the largest natural swamps in the world. The Jonglei canal

---

Background: Sudan

Rarely in the past two centuries has Sudan known peace and stability. Under British administration (1898—1955) the troubled south was violently pacified, but economic stagnation and British policy stored up problems for the future: in the north the British promoted Islam as a unifying force among the predominantly Arab peoples, while the south, the majority of whose black African people are not Muslims, was administered separately.

Sudan became independent in 1956. The south was under-represented in government, and in 1963 the "Anya-Nya" movement for southern independence was formed and civil war broke out. The first civil war ended with the Addis Ababa agreement of 1972, establishing a single regional government in the south. President Nimeiri then attempted to give the south more political power, but violent northern opposition coupled with economic crisis forced him, in 1977, to abandon this policy.

In 1983, the south was redivided into three regions, and Islamic 'sharia' law was declared valid in the whole of Sudan. War was renewed as the Sudan People's Liberation Army (SPLA) emerged to fight for a fairer place for the south in Sudan's political and economic structure. SPLA demands include the withdrawal of Islamic law and a constitutional conference.

Nimeiri's government fell in 1985. During the following period of parliamentary rule, various attempts were made to initiate peace talks with the SPLA. These ended with the military coup of June 1989, which brought Omar El Beshir to power, backed by the National Islamic Front. Islamic law was confirmed as applying to the whole of Sudan in January 1991.

would partially drain the swamp, and water saved from evaporation would be used to irrigate an extra 1.2 to 1.6 million hectares of land in central Sudan, and a similar area in Egypt. The plan proposed to drain or reduce the swamp area by about 20%, and to increase the Nile flow through the new canal by 10-15 billion cubic metres a year [5]. The canal would also greatly speed up river transport from Khartoum to Juba, the main city in the south.

Seen from the northern reaches of the Nile, the Sudd seems an enormous waste of a shared natural resource. But for the million people living in this ecosystem, mostly Dinka and Nuer pastoralists, the Sudd is their source of life. Their cattle graze throughout the region during the flood season, while during the dry months they graze on the banks of the Nile. These flood plains are the major cattle-producing areas of the region, and any change in the water level would have significant impact on the economy.

The canal scheme was also supposed to aid southern Sudan by upgrading 1.5 million hectares of agricultural land and opening it up to modern agriculture. Critics of the scheme say that there is no shortage of cultivable land in the region; estimates put the proportion of arable land under cultivation at only 12%. A better starting point for aiding southern Sudan, they say, would be to harness existing potential, not to open up new land [6].

Many southern Sudanese have viewed the Jonglei canal scheme as exploitative. It has always been strongly opposed by the rural population of the Nile tribes and has had a great impact on the current war in the south. It became a symbol of SPLA protest in 1983, and was one of their principal targets when war broke out, in Bor, where the canal should have started. Digging has been suspended ever since, although more than half the canal has already been excavated.

The current war is a result of the frustration of the people of the south, who have been ignored in development. Southern Sudan is potentially the richest part of the country. It has a much higher percentage of rainfall, most of the natural forests, most of the rivers, streams, fish and wildlife, and there is much mineral wealth waiting to be extracted. Many industrial projects have been proposed for the south but never implemented: rice and sugar plantations, textile production, gold mines, hydro-electric schemes, a paper factory and fishing projects.

The 1972 Addis Ababa agreement brought the fighting in the

south to a halt. But uneven development and under-investment in the south continue and war broke out again in 1982. One of the main objectives of the Sudan People's Liberation Movement (SPLM) is that national resources should be shared and development schemes should benefit the south, not solely the north—which is how the southern Sudanese view the outcome of the Jonglei canal project.

The cost of war

The budget devoted to the Sudanese armed forces is ten times that allocated to development projects. In 1989/90, the Sudanese government suspended some sections of the development budget. The agricultural and industrial sectors were on the point of collapse, starved of funds which have been spent on the war.

Poverty in the south has increased because of the terrible damage inflicted by the war on people, the infrastructure and the environment. Some 75% of the Dinka and the Nuer have been displaced from their homes along the River Nile, and they have lost several million head of cattle.

Despite its great natural resources and therefore its potential for development, Sudan today is known for its political instability, poverty, famines and refugees, all of them the result of wars and the mismanagement of the country's natural resources. So far the government has refused to cancel the agreement to allow Egypt to exploit the water of the Jonglei canal. Peace discussions should take into account the development needs of the south, which means agreements over access to and shared benefit from resources.

CHAPTER SIX

Social Breakdown

> In the old days I was a farmer and had animals. I was master
> of myself, maintaining economic self-sufficiency. Then the war
> came.... Now I am a beggar. Because of the poverty many people
> have turned into armed robbers, and theft has visibly
> increased.
> *Girmay Gerbray, from Tigray and Eritrea, now living in Sudan*

Communities caught up in violent conflict suffer in many ways. War
causes individual deaths and injury, as well as material destruction,
but it may also weaken or destroy people's sense of communal
identity. Environmental changes which destroy a community's
economic viability can have similar effects. Social and cultural
traditions, built up over generations around a particular way of life
in a particular region, begin to lose their meaning. Pastoralists, for
example, who can no longer live by herding, may become socially
alienated as well as materially destitute. Farming communities who
helped each other in times of need may find, as conditions worsen,
that family and village solidarity breaks down.

Berhane Woldegabriel, an Eritrean journalist based in
Khartoum, continues the story of the Lahawin in east Sudan (see
Chapter Three) with an account of the attacks from bandits, the
faloul, along the border between Sudan and Ethiopia, which pose a
further threat to the pastoralists' way of life. The principal cause of
the alienation of the *faloul* was displacement resulting from war,
but the simultaneous dearth of natural resources because of drought
made it even harder for them to settle and become self-sufficient.
Drought, too, forces the Lahawin to take their herds into the richer
border areas where they become more vulnerable to attack. The

faloul are desperate, and fighting for survival. Their numbers are growing, and as the border areas are already caught up in wars, they are increasingly beyond the reach of the law.

Rule by the gun
by Berhane Woldegabriel

The outlaw groups are referred to by various names. Originally these terms specified different types of outlaw, but increasingly nowadays, as the activities of the various groups escalate and merge, the names are used indiscriminately.

The general term is *shifta*, defined in the modern Tigrinya dictionary as "one who is a rebel, an outlaw who lives in the forests and exists by force and robbery". The word originally had a more precise and noble meaning, and as such it has an honourable place in Ethiopian history. It meant a Robin Hood figure who stood against social injustice, particularly against wrongs perpetrated against himself, a member of his family or clan, by government authorities or a village chief. The *shifta* would live in the forests until he had redressed the wrong, robbing from the rich to distribute among the poor, gathering followers and supported by peasants.

Background: the Sudanese-Ethiopian border area

Along the border between Sudan and Ethiopia, relationships between the various groups are tangled, tense and often violent. There are pastoralists affected by drought, crossing the border to compete for resources with other nomadic and local groups; there are members of Eritrean and Tigrayan liberation movements, fighting the Ethiopian government and needing access from Sudan to the territory they control inside Ethiopia; and there are refugees from these wars, from battles between the different liberation fronts eg the Eritrean Liberation Front versus the Eritrean People's Liberation Front (see Chapter Eight, p132), and from drought and famine. Some of the border areas, which were never thoroughly under the control of the Ethiopian government, are now in the hands of the liberation movements; others are disputed. Years of fighting, lack of government control, and drought have created an area of social breakdown, violence and lawlessness. Groups of dislocated and uprooted people live by banditry and the gun, attacking traders or taking rich merchants, farmers and nomads hostage for ransom. Firearms are plentiful in the region, which makes the violence more deadly.

The exploits of the *shifta* are celebrated in poetry. In feudal Ethiopia and Eritrea inherited power was often abused, and the *shifta* were at times a check and balance to the activities of the autocratic government.

Some *shifta* (using the word in its modern, lesser meaning) are also known as *faloul*. This second term used to be a social one, referring to an adolescent boy who defied his parents, and displayed socially unacceptable behaviour such as smoking or spending the night away from home.

The war in Ethiopia between the government and the Eritrean liberation movement, and conflict between various Eritrean factions, produced a new use of the word *faloul*. In 1977 a group broke away from one of the Eritrean organisations, the Eritrean Liberation Front (ELF). The ELF referred to the splinter group as *faloul*, meaning in this case anarchists, people who refused to accept organisation (although a politically minded group of them did in fact call themselves the Eritrean Democratic Movement). When in 1981 the ELF was defeated and driven into Sudan by the coordinated forces of the Eritrean People's Liberation Front (EPLF) and the Tigrayan People's Liberation Front (TPLF), these *faloul* found themselves caught along the Sudan-Eritrea border without financial support or military or political leadership, in a period of severe drought. Thousands of fighters left Eritrea for Sudan, abandoning or selling their arms as they left. Others, mostly young men, became a new generation of *shifta*, following military discipline and equipped with modern guns, radio communications and maps.

The third type of outlaw are the *kafagne*. *Kafagne* is an Amharic word meaning "discontented". It seems that the *kafagne* were originally peasants, who left their villages to follow their feudal lords who had been ousted in the 1974 revolution, to fight against the Dergue (the revolutionary military junta) and later the Ethiopian People's Revolutionary Party (EPRP). They also fought against other anti-right wing forces, such as the TPLF. Gradually these peasants became disenchanted—*kafagne*—with their feudal leaders, and confused by the conflicting interests and forces between which they were caught. They do not seem to have any political objective, but are condemned to live as *shifta* because they are surrounded by enemies. They cannot join any of the established powers in the region because at one time or another they have fought against all of them. The Ethiopian government has not sought to subdue and control them because they fought against the government's enemies, particularly the TPLF, and because they do not present a serious threat to the state's power, only to the pastoralists in the area. Since mid-1990, however, some *faloul* are allegedly being used by the government against the TPLF, along the border with Sudan. In December 1990 there were some skirmishes between the TPLF and the Sudanese border army, triggered by the activities of the *faloul*.

The vulnerability of pastoralists

All these outlaws, now commonly described as *faloul*, prey on the pastoralists. Why do the herdsmen, particularly the Lahawin, lay themselves open to attack? Because drought on the Sudanese side forces them to cross into border territory, where the land is richer. The chief of the Lahawin said that since the drought years the type of grass which has been growing in their traditional rangelands is not suitable for animals. The drought caused the useful types of natural vegetation to recede at the same time as the animal population was growing and the land available for grazing was shrinking. So the Lahawin have been forced to enter Eritrea and Ethiopia, even though some of the suitable grazing land has been mined and they are vulnerable to air bombardment from the Ethiopian military.

"The type of vegetation, the weather and the availability of water in those areas attract the Lahawin and Shukriya nomads. The sun shines more gently there, the people and animals walk from the shade of one tree to the next, the grass is tall and lush, giving scent and shade. The thinnest cow gets fat and gives birth to a calf. So come what may, we will continue to cross the border," said one pastoralist about their dangerous dry-season migrations.

Lahawin protest

For centuries the Lahawin have been pastoralists. Now many are having to seek a sedentary way of life to survive. The Lahawin asked the Sudanese government to give them land where they could settle, and they were allocated an area near Wad el Hileau in Maharegat. However, when they started to build houses, police came and stopped them. This apparent reversal of the government's decision so infuriated the Lahawin that some of them beat up one of the policemen. The Lahawin have a reputation of rarely resorting to

Neil Cooper/Panos Pictures

In areas of insecurity, violence breeds violence as people, like these Afar salt traders, take up arms as protection against bandits and outlaws.

violence and this incident indicates their rising discontent and desperation, as does the fact that they are now said to be armed. All but one of the Lahawin interviewed for *Greenwar* were of the opinion that the government in Khartoum is pursuing a deliberate policy of making life more and more difficult for them.

As Berhane Woldegabriel explains, local people feel the large numbers of refugees in the Sudanese-Ethiopian border area compete with them for resources and jobs. In the tense atmosphere of the troubled region, it is not only *faloul* who resort to violence and armed robbery but also, on occasion, local people.

Yohannes' story

Yohannes is a Tigrayan refugee who has lived in Sudan for eight years, making his living during the rainy and harvesting months as a hired labourer on the big mechanised farms in the Semsem area west of Gedaref town. He has been subjected on several occasions to attacks by local groups he calls "Arabs", meaning nomads of various tribes but primarily the Massalit. The Massalit wish to scare the refugees away from these areas of potential employment and have gained a bloodthirsty reputation.

Yohannes is stoical about the dangers to himself and other refugee farm labourers. "It has always been the same, ever since I came to Sudan. I only work in the Semsem area because the area east of Gedaref is too dangerous. But now, even in Semsem, it is getting bad. Sometimes when we are working in the fields, and we have left our few things in the field huts, the Arabs come and steal all we have. This has happened to me several times over the years."

In February 1990, Yohannes was working in the Kosema area of Semsem. He recalls the time he thought he was going to die: "It was seven in the morning, and two of us were walking along the road, heading back to Gedaref as our work had ended. Four *Arab el Khalla'a* [Arabs who are not settled] came up to us on their camels. They demanded our money and possessions, but we only had a change of clothes, our watches and a few pounds. I put my hand in my bag and pretended I had a pistol. They got out their whips, and so I handed over my watch and clothes but threatened to shoot them if they did not go. By chance a lorry came by. The driver told the Arabs to kill us, but they were frightened as they believed I had a gun. I was so angry, I was ready to kill or die. But I had no way of killing, it's just that I'm tall and strong. After a while they rode off."

Asked if he told the farmer who hired him about the attack, he replies, "Yes, but he just laughed and said, 'OK, we'll buy you pistols so that you can really kill them.' But refugees cannot carry guns in Sudan, it is too dangerous."

Guns instead of land

War has not affected Senegal so severely as it has many other countries of the Sahel. But decades of drought and mismanaged rural development have reduced much of the rural population to poverty and forced many of them to abandon agriculture and seek other ways of surviving, as Senegalese journalist **Babacar Touré** explains.

"The English run": smuggling in Senegal
by Babacar Touré

Mbage is about 26 years old. Originally from Ndengueler, a small village in the groundnut growing area in the centre of Senegal, he went to try his luck in Dakar, the capital, three years ago. He lives there with his brother, a government official. Recently he confided to his brother: "I know it's not easy for you, but even so I'd like to ask you to help. Things aren't going well in the village because the soil is exhausted, so I'd like to try the English run. I know it's hell down there, but warriors can always get through."

This is coded language. For the uninitiated: "the English run" refers to The Gambia, while the "warriors" are the thousands of smugglers, occasional or professional, who buy goods in The Gambia, especially textiles, sugar, tea and cosmetics, for re-sale in Senegal. The language of the trade is heavily laced with phrases of war.

Mbage's village is far from the Gambian border but everyone in the area knows of "the English run", and is confident that The Gambia is an inexhaustible source of wealth; all you need is courage and "a few tricks in order to line your pockets". Such smuggling is not a recent phenomenon, but today it is on the increase. Peasants as well as the town-dwellers of Saloum and Baol have turned in droves to the illicit trade because the land is no longer fruitful.

The Senegalese state was never keen on the fact that the territory of The Gambia enclosed within it had more flexible fiscal arrangements. These allowed it to become a kind of hypermarket, whose biggest clients were Senegal's own nationals. Products from every country flood into Senegal via Banjul, The Gambia's capital. The Gambia represents a threat to the Senegalese economy. This is why, when in 1981 armed rebels tried to take power from President Jawara of The Gambia, Senegal seized the chance and sent its army to support him. Some forgotten agreements were dusted off and used to legalise this intervention in retrospect.

Dakar and Banjul, on The Gambia's initiative, then signed a Confederal Pact, one of whose prime aims, as far as Senegal was concerned, was to harmonise monetary and customs policies in order to put an end to smuggling. Realising what was at stake and recognising the threat to their wallets, Gambian businessmen put pressure on their government and finally succeeded in breaking up the confederation in 1989.

Since then, Dakar has sought to "seal off" The Gambia with an impressive customs barrier in order "to save the economy", according to the Senegalese Director-General of Customs, Mouhamadou Moustapha Tall. Such moves are dismissed as "a waste of time" by Mansour, a man from Kaolack who is well-versed in smuggling. "The state can heighten surveillance of the border posts if it likes, but people who make their living from the trade will not give up....What does the government expect? There are no jobs, people are being put out of work, the land is no longer fruitful, but we have to live. So, even if it costs them their lives, smugglers will not be intimidated."

Indeed it does cost lives, those of customs officers as well as smugglers. On well-hidden tracks or on the river, in the depths of night, the outlaws play hide-and-seek with the "guardians of the economy". Kaolack, the capital of the groundnut-growing region and buffer area between The Gambia and the rest of Senegal, resembles the American Wild West. Shoot-outs have happened more than once in the middle of the town, between fleeing smugglers and pursuing customs officers.

Outside the town it is no better. Some Senegalese customs officers believe that certain villages are "no-go" areas where it would be dangerous to pursue a smuggler. They keep on asking for more and more sophisticated weapons from a government which apparently heeds their calls.

The debate was opened up again in May 1990, following an attack with automatic weapons on a Senegalese customs post at Séléty on the Gambian border which left two customs officials dead.

On several occasions, wildlife and forest wardens as well as customs officials in Senegal's eastern region have seized weapons from individuals. Poaching in the Niokolo Koba national park (the largest nature reserve in Senegal, covering 1 million hectares) has become the main source of income for local people devastated by the years of drought. Places like Medina Gounass are said to be "refuges for poachers". The annual religious festival in Medina is the occasion for an immense trade in arms. Smugglers and poachers meet up there, now convinced that "when the land is no longer fruitful and the authorities have abandoned us peasants, we can only survive by using guns". It is also by the use of guns that they often die. At certain times of the year, the huge park becomes an area of guerilla warfare, far from any witnesses.

The prospect that these skirmishes might escalate is a frightening one. The pursuit of smugglers and poachers could exceed the limits acceptable to the states concerned, or weapons seizures at border posts might point the finger of suspicion at neighbouring governments. No one knows how many weapons have reached Senegal clandestinely during the last few years, let alone for whom they are destined. Yet the killings which have multiplied since 1980 leave one thing beyond doubt: the rifles were not purchased to decorate the living-room.

The vicious circle

The kind of incidents described in this chapter rarely involve large numbers of deaths. They tend to take place among scattered groups, away from the public eye, and cause sporadic but continual casualties. The result is a culture of violence and lawlessness, which is pervasive and undermining, and rapidly takes hold in a disrupted and insecure area. As **Berhane Woldegabriel**'s interview with a police chief in east Sudan shows, children growing up in this atmosphere all too easily adapt to such a culture in order to survive. And so the social disruption is reinforced from one generation to the next.

Young bandits
by Berhane Woldegabriel

Wad el Hileau village is in east Sudan, near the Ethiopian border, and contains more than 18,000 refugees and Sudanese nationals.

Children growing up in an atmosphere of violence and lawlessness all too easily adapt to such a culture in order to survive.

The Wad el Hileau police chief says that one of his main problems concerns refugee children, particularly those aged 12 to 14 years. They usually come from families where the mother is the head of the household and the father is absent, either fighting in one of the liberation struggles, working in Sudanese cities, agricultural schemes or the Gulf countries, or dead.

Mulu Abdel Gardir is a 34-year-old woman of the Jiberti tribe, a Muslim refugee from the highlands of Tigray in Ethiopia. Together with her elder sister, she owns a small tea shop in Wad el Hileau. Her husband left her and their three children in 1989, in response to a call by the Tigrayan People's Liberation Front (TPLF) to fight the Ethiopian government. In May 1990, the oldest child, a boy aged 13, was taken into police custody for stealing. He had been assisted by five friends, all refugee children. "Two of these boys have fathers who are *kafagne*," said Sergeant Osman, who is concerned that the children are growing up to be urban *shifta*. In Wad el Hileau village alone, he knows of about 150 refugee children engaged in petty and serious criminal activities.

CHAPTER SEVEN

Displacement

> Let my stomach burn from hunger but let me never leave my country.
> *Teslem mt Magha, refugee, Mauritania*

Seasonal migration has long been an integral part of life for many Sahelians. Today, the intensification of conflict over resources means that migration is increasingly no longer a matter of individual choice. People are being driven from their lands because the environment will no longer support them, and because of communal instability and violence. In some instances governments have deliberately resettled their citizens, as a means of easing the pressure on over-populated land.

Some of these people cross national boundaries and are classified as refugees, others remain within their country and are defined as displaced. But the problems resulting from this Greenwar factor are the same: homelessness, loss of livelihood, and cultural dislocation.

Whatever the causes, displacement is itself a kind of violence— violence to the refugees and the displaced themselves, and violence to the people, resources and economies of the areas to which they are forced to move. An influx of refugees increases the pressure on the surrounding environment, which can lead to tension between the new settlers and the local population, and so to the possibility of further conflict. Individuals suffer the violent psychological trauma of being uprooted and forced to re-establish themselves in alien, overcrowded and difficult surroundings. As Sudanese journalist **Nafissa Abdel Rahim** discovered in Sudan, the consequences can be particularly severe for children and for women, whose lives are often more closely circumscribed by cultural traditions than those of men.

Disrupted lives, changing traditions
by Nafissa Abdel Rahim

Sudan, in common with most Sahelian countries, has suffered prolonged periods of extensive drought since the late 1960s. The first to suffer from the deteriorating situation were the small farmers and poorer pastoralists. Many, in desperation, migrated to Sudan's larger urban centres. In 1984-85, for example, nearly 3 million people were displaced by drought. Over 4 million more were uprooted from the southern regions, because of the civil war and the intertribal disputes in Kordofan, Darfur and elsewhere. Altogether, Sudan has an estimated 7 million displaced, out of a total population of about 24 million.

The ratio of children, women and men among the displaced in Sudan is 3:2:1 respectively, which shows the burden women are shouldering. Many women are supporting their families alone, because their husbands either have migrated to other areas in search of work or, as in many cases, have more than one wife and cannot take care of them all, particularly in the deteriorating economic situation.

Most of the displaced have settled near Khartoum and other urban centres, in camps or in shanty towns. Some have coped more successfully than others with the social and economic upheaval. Those coming originally from small towns were at an advantage, but for nomad tribes and other groups from the rural areas—who constitute the majority of the displaced—adapting to town life was much more difficult. While the city represented for them a certain degree of security from the privations of war and drought, many found it hard to adapt to differences in traditions and customs, and to the economic pressures. This is most clearly seen in the situations of women and children.

Awiel's story

Awiel Mano is in her thirties, but she looks much older. She is from the south, the area around Bentiu in the Upper Nile region, and since 1989 has lived in Hillat Shook, a settlement which grew up south of Khartoum. The camp has a population of 20,000, consisting of people from southern and western Sudan [1]. Awiel lives with her husband and five children in a shelter made of sacks tied around a framework of branches.

At home in Bentiu she had been very active. Her day would start early with the collection of water and firewood for cooking. Having ground her *dura* (sorghum) at home, as the mill was some kilometres away, she would prepare a meal for her children, and then follow her husband to their farm to work on the land.

One day Awiel's village was raided by members of the Sudan People's Liberation Army (SPLA). Their cattle were stolen and her husband was injured but he survived. Following this incident, and along with many others, they moved to Khartoum. They stayed at first in a camp near the industrial part of Khartoum. However, living conditions were bad and they soon moved to Hillat Shook. It is a better camp but densely crowded and strewn with rubbish; disease spreads fast, particularly as there are not enough latrines.

Awiel tried to get work washing and cleaning in some of the capital's houses but discovered that her earnings were not enough to sustain her and her children, whom she left alone all day. Her children received some milk from a supplementary feeding programme carried out by one of the local non-governmental organisations (NGOs). This programme was only reaching 12.2% of the malnourished children in the camp, whose numbers are still moderately high [2]. Malnutrition among pregnant women is also a problem and it seems likely that mothers give most of the food to their husband and children, saving relatively little for themselves.

The stresses of life in the crowded camps have broken down or changed many tribal traditions and customs. There are many widows with nobody to care for them: a new phenomenon arising from the disintegration of the family network and the wider social structure. In the south, when a husband dies his male relatives take care of his widow and children and their financial needs. "Now, in Khartoum, everybody is just thinking about himself and how to sustain his own family," remarked one of the women. And she continued with an example of how hard it is becoming to maintain the ceremonies which bind families together: "To make a *karama* (sacrifice) is very difficult now. My sister could not make a *karama* for her newborn child so that God may protect him and to drive away the evil spirits, because we could not afford to buy a goat or a sheep."

Clashes of custom can cause problems, too. Awiel comes from the south, where brewing and drinking beer is quite common, especially for certain ceremonies. "I started making local beer and was getting a good income from it. This helped when my husband was not working, but the people who came to drink made a lot of noise and residents living near the camp complained to the police. My pots were confiscated and I was warned not to repeat this." It was difficult for her to understand that brewing alcohol is unacceptable in the Muslim north, where traditions are different and women working in such professions are socially despised.

Children suffer a lot from the new way of life. Most now work in marginal activities, such as selling water, cigarettes, fruit and bananas in the streets. A high proportion of vagrant children in the capital are from displaced families. Because they needed to work, most of them have lost the chance of being educated.

Awiel's son Deing is only 10 and ought to be at school, but she has to send him out to work. His father does not like the idea but has to accept the situation, particularly since he himself is not working most of the time. He used to sell fish, which he would get from the nearby central market, but after the prices were raised, his small profit margin disappeared. He tried to find work in the construction industry but the shortage of cement and other materials means jobs are rarely available.

Deing is a tall boy who tries to seem older than his age, but sometimes his childlike naughtiness betrays him. "I was studying in the fourth year in the south. My father wanted me to go to school and used to be angry if I played during school hours. We used to have 50 cows. My brothers and I looked after them. Then all the cows were taken away and our house was burnt down. I do not want to go to school here because I want to help my father who is not working."

Changes

The collapse of old traditions can sometimes be positive. Contact with urban life is creating a growing interest in education and health care. Families who can afford it are taking more interest in sending boys to school. Girls, however, tend to be kept in the house to help their mothers, and may be married before they are even 12.

Among cow-owning tribes it was the custom to give many cows as a dowry for marriage, which made affording marriage very difficult after the rise in livestock prices. There was also the complication after divorce of having to return cows. Among the displaced, dowries are now being paid in cash, although some insist that the man promise to pay the rest of the dowry in cows when he returns to the south.

"One positive change emerging is that men now cannot often afford to marry more than one wife, as it is difficult to support several families," commented Awiel.

Environmental pressures

When the displaced came to the capital, like Awiel they were settled in places which were originally industrial areas and dumping grounds for waste. Because relief efforts have concentrated on food, medicines or clothes, the issue of environmental health has received less attention.

Water remains scarce despite the efforts of the Commission of the Displaced and of NGOs to install water containers in the camps. Sometimes people pay 3-5 Sudanese pounds (about US 60 cents— US$1) for a tin of water which barely provides enough for drinking, let alone washing, cooking and cleaning.

Another problem is access to firewood. Collection of wood and water are traditionally women's responsibilities. In this sense, women directly assist the desertification process. Their desperate situation, however, makes it difficult for them to gain access to education and knowledge about the risk of desertification, let alone change their practice.

It has become commonplace in Khartoum and adjacent Omdurman to see lines of displaced women carrying back to the camps great bundles of dry and green wood on their heads. From the dust covering their legs and the tired look on their faces, it is clear that they have walked great distances to get this firewood; all nearby supplies have been exhausted. Thus the deforestation which took place in west and east Sudan, and other areas affected by drought, is now being repeated around Khartoum. Charcoal prices are high and national efforts to promote the use of energy-efficient stoves have yet to make much impact, so firewood remains the cheapest form of energy for these women. As well as the wood cut for fuel, a great deal of wood is needed to build the shelters in the camps.

Fatima's story

Fatima is a middle-aged woman from one of the Cabalish nomad tribes, who were displaced from west Sudan. She came eight years ago from Sodari district in North Kordofan, which has the highest outflow of displaced people. Following a three-year drought,

Fatima's people had lost their cattle; they had consumed all their reserves of *dura*; and their *dukhun* (maize) cultivation had failed. Fatima has settled at Wad el Beshir camp, west of Omdurman, which is inhabited by different tribes from south and west Sudan. She has six children and lives with her elder daughter, her daughter's husband and their two children.

Many rural Sudanese women in the west, south and some parts of north and central Sudan are used to working in agriculture, construction and some retail businesses. But there are some communities in which women's activities are limited to work inside the home. For them, adapting to their new situation as the displaced is even more difficult.

After eight years, Fatima still has not adjusted to life in Khartoum. When describing how she used to live, before the drought, she explained that men used to do everything. They would take the cattle for grazing, and get all the household supplies. She was not even supposed to go out and collect the firewood; she was responsible only for preparing food. "Most of the time we were inside our homes, we did not go outside except for urgent matters. We did not know what was going on inside our closest neighbour's shelter.

"Now a lot of things have changed. Women are leaving their families and children all the time. Some of our young girls are spoiled by the city life and they no longer want to live the way we used to. They say they want to be educated and have an easier, less isolated life."

Breaking cultural traditions

Women of the Beja nomad tribe are also not accustomed to moving outside the home. Traditionally, they prepared food and made the *birish* (woven palm leaves) from which their homes are constructed. Everything else was considered men's work. The pattern of life changed drastically after the 1984-85 drought. The Beja, strongly attached to their land, were particularly affected.

The deterioration of the environment and of grazing resources, especially in the 1984-85 drought, caused the death of many of their cattle, and limited their freedom of movement. In 1985 50,000 Beja were compelled to settle near towns such as Sinkat and Tahamiyam, along the Khartoum-Port Sudan highway. Many of the men left their families to look for work in Port Sudan or Kassala, in the hope that

Sarah Errington/Hutchison Library

Beja women at a wedding. Displaced families often have to live with the humiliation of being unable to maintain their traditional culture.

they would earn enough to replace their lost livestock and resume their traditional way of life. Most are still working away from their families.

The Beja tradition of tribal collectivism, which considers the man responsible for women, dependents and guests, placed these displaced women in a particularly difficult position. Custom maintains that they should stay at home; there is no understanding of a woman working, however poor she is.

Mayo is one of the shanty towns which has been growing up since the early 1970s around Sinkat, 120 km south of Port Sudan, and which expanded with the influx of displaced from the 1984-85 drought. Women headed approximately 51% of the households in Mayo, either because the men were away working in Port Sudan, Toker and Kassala, or because the women were divorced, widowed or deserted. It used to be unusual for Beja men to desert or divorce their wives, but when they realised that it was impossible for them to fulfil their traditional tribal responsibilities towards their families, many of them opted out. Women who in the past were totally dependent on their husbands now have to work like men to support themselves, their children and often a mother or an aunt.

The fact that the Beja have the same ethnic origins as Sinkat inhabitants highlights their problem of having broken with tribal tradition, which is why these displaced women are so reluctant to talk about their work. They feel different to other Beja women. Much Beja poetry is concerned with female beauty (Beja women are considered among the most beautiful in Sudan), describing their slim soft bodies, their smooth long necks. One poet praises his lover's soft hands, so delicate that they would be affected by merely shaking another's. The image of women is that they are polite and gentle with large, pure eyes twinkling "like the morning star".

Such descriptions certainly no longer apply to the poor malnourished women in Mayo today, who feel they have become almost like men, because they come from a society which does not approve of the work they do. Even after seven or eight years in a settlement, the women, particularly the young ones, are not expected to walk through the marketplace, let alone work in it. The market is still considered the men's domain, where they sell firewood, charcoal, *dura*, ghee, milk and skins. Most women do not have the courage to sell their wares—palm leaf mats, food, boiled eggs, sweets and toothbrushes (from the Arak tree, *Salvadora persica*). Instead, they send their children or old women to sell their goods not only in the market, but also along the highway or at the railway station.

What they earn is often not enough to cover their basic needs. Most women are producing the same things, so supply exceeds demand and prices have dropped. Many of their children look malnourished. Their diet used to consist of milk, *dura* and dates. Now their families cannot afford milk so the children often eat their *dura* porridge mixed with oil, and sometimes only water.

Future prospects

The Beja traditionally place great value on trees. Cutting of green trees is prohibited, and even throwing stones at a tree to knock down its fruits is not acceptable. Beja clans allow strangers from other tribes to graze their animals on Beja land but do not allow them to cut the trees. Much of their poetry is also about the environment. A famous poet described the green trees surrounding a *khor* (river) as the *rasiel* (ornaments) decorating a woman's neck.

Will the Beja women ever again be able to inhale the pure air on the top of the mountain and taste the sweet water, and return to the mountain like "a thirsty sheep going back to its flock"?

This depends on the success of government plans to rehabilitate the forests in the Red Sea Hills area (see map in Chapter Three, p44). The province has already lost almost 70% of its forest. This is in part due to problems of land ownership, and also to the increased consumption of fuel in urban centres following the growth in their populations. Port Sudan, the province's capital, grew from 132,632 in 1973 to 350,000 by 1983.

The success of these reforestation plans depends in turn on the extent to which they incorporate people's participation, and on how much effort is put into developing other sources of income. Marketing firewood and charcoal has a long tradition among the Beja, but after the drought and with the deteriorating economy, a growing number of families became involved in charcoal-burning. This has become an even more important source of income, and tree-felling has increased correspondingly.

Relocation: a deliberate stategy

In Ethiopia, the government has resettled some 600,000 people, in an attempt to relieve the pressure on over-cultivated and exhausted lands in the mountainous north of the country. New settlements were hastily established in less densely populated areas in the south. Critics condemn the force which has been used, and argue that such planned movements of populations cannot on their own be seen as solutions to the problems of environmental degradation in the Sahel, because the resettlement itself raises new difficulties and conflicts. Ethiopian writer **Tafesse Hailu** takes a critical look at the controversial programme.

Resettlement: kill or cure?
by Tafesse Hailu

The history of famine in Ethiopia goes back for centuries. The first historically documented famine occurred during the thirteenth century, and Ethiopia has been struck by cyclical famine ever since.

The recent severe famines in 1974-75, 1984-85 and 1990-91 occurred primarily as a result of droughts, but the impact of these droughts has been magnified because they affected agricultural areas which were already suffering from serious environmental degradation and reduced productivity.

Wollo, Tigray and the highlands of Eritrea have been most affected. These regions have experienced a long period of human settlement and over-utilisation of land, while population growth (approximately 3% a year) was increasing the pressure on the already denuded highlands [3]. As more and more trees were cut for fuelwood and building materials, the hillsides became more vulnerable to the heavy seasonal rains which wash away the soil in torrents.

The 1974-75 famine caused death and suffering to millions of Ethiopians. It was known as the "hidden famine", because the government of Emperor Haile Selassie tried to conceal information about it to avoid damaging world opinion about developments in Ethiopia. A British television journalist, Jonathan Dimbleby, travelled secretly to the drought-striken regions. When his film was screened in Europe, it revealed the extent of the starvation and suffering. The monarchy was discredited, and the 1974-75 famine was one of the prime causes of the downfall of Haile Selassie and his government.

The origins of the programme

The new revolutionary regime, the Dergue, under President Mengistu Haile Mariam, which toppled Haile Selassie's government in September 1974, had to tackle the problems of drought and famine as a matter of urgency. It believed strongly that resettlement—moving farmers from the overcrowded hillsides of the famine-affected regions to less densely populated areas further south—would provide a "lasting solution". At first this policy was justified solely as the logical response to the immediate problem of mass starvation; later, longer-term issues of population pressure,

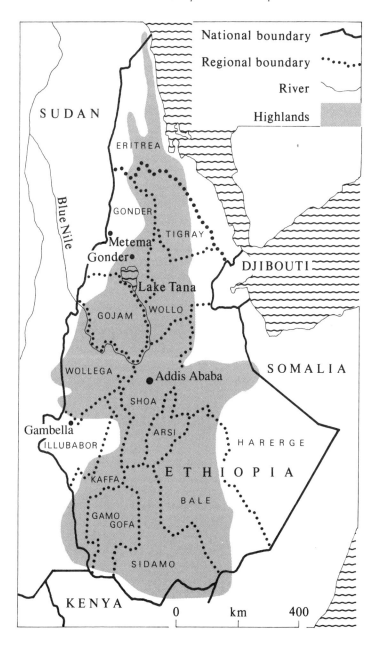

National boundary

Regional boundary

River

Highlands

SUDAN

ERITREA

Blue Nile

GONDER

Metema

TIGRAY

Gonder

DJIBOUTI

Lake Tana

WOLLO

GOJAM

WOLLEGA

Addis Ababa

SOMALIA

SHOA

Gambella

ARSI

ILLUBABOR

HARERGE

KAFFA

E T H I O P I A

BALE

GAMO
GOFA

SIDAMO

KENYA

0   km   400

and the improvement of land use and food production were introduced as major justifications.

Dr Dessalegn Rahmato, assistant professor in the Institute of Development Research, Addis Ababa, and an expert on resettlement, has written of the Ethiopian government's policy: "The country's resettlement programme is in deep crisis; bedevilled, among other things, by low settler morale, high rates of desertion, poor economic performance, and soaring costs [4]."

The famine of 1984-85, again particularly in the northern regions, namely Eritrea, Tigray and Wollo, gave further impetus to the government's resettlement programme.

Background: Eritrea and Tigray

These areas, it should be noted, are at war with the government in Addis, with groups fighting either for independence (Eritrea) or for a different, more representative form of government (Tigray). Some participants and observers have alleged that the resettlement programme was motivated as much by the political need to move populations out of the rebel areas, as by the desire to improve the environmental and economic conditions of settlers and the people remaining behind.

Overall, the famine affected almost 10 million people. A serious reduction in rainfall over large parts of Ethiopia in 1984 led to a shortfall of about 20% of agricultural production—a loss of about 1 million tonnes, mainly of cereals and pulses. As a result the resettlement programme was greatly accelerated.

An official of the Co-operatives Service Department in the Relief and Rehabilitation Commission (RRC) said: "Before the famine, the RRC masterplan was to settle 14,000 families in several parts of the country over the coming few years. But in November 1984, government leaders announced emergency plans to relocate 500,000 families (or about 2 million people) from northern Ethiopia to other parts of the country, less densely settled and more viable agriculturally. So the Central Planning Committee and RRC had to make hasty preparations."

The authorities selected resettlement areas in Wollega, Illubabor and Kaffa, the three southwestern administrative regions of the country. Resettlement sites were selected and prepared in great haste. Dr Dessalegn Rahmato says: "The project in Metekel province, Gojam region, was launched without any proper feasibility studies. In fact, the selection of settlement sites in Metekel was made by local authorities on the basis of brief helicopter flights over the province. Furthermore, almost all of the new projects hastily opened up were located in hot and semi-arid lowland areas infested with malaria, trypanosomiasis, yellow fever and other endemic diseases, to which highland peasants have no immunity [5]."

The government target was to move 1.5 million people, but the problems encountered meant that by October 1985 only just over 0.5 million had been moved [6]. Ato Meheret Ayenew, a lecturer at the College of Social Science, Addis Ababa University, has studied some of the consequences of the emergency resettlement programme. "The movement of people to new resettlement sites was plagued by confusion, disorganisation and mismanagement. To take so many people to places 1,000 km away at a time when they were nutritionally weak and suffering the trauma of famine and dislocation was an imprudent act. Not only did the government show lack of understanding of transport logistics—it demonstrated a total insensitivity to human beings.

"Misery and suffering characterised the entire resettlement operation. This was because there was no prior planning or preparation. In consequence, there was coercion and fragmentation of families in the recruitment process, poor feeding and health facilities in transit, shortages of relief goods and inadequate—even non-existent—land use planning in the reception areas, and coercive management practices in resettlement areas. Many resettlement sites were unsuitable as they were later found to be habitats of diseases like malaria, and of the tsetse fly. There was also little or no knowledge of the carrying capacity of land or the soil fertility."

Selection of settlers

How were settlers selected or screened? The methods used to recruit candidates varied widely from place to place. However, in most cases, they were not based on voluntary consent, nor were they free and fair. An experienced field staff member, now with the Public Relations Office of the RRC, confided: "Selection committees used forceful or unethical methods in a large number of places. Peasants were either rounded up and sent to transit camps, or falsely enticed into the programme. In Wollo, for example, the local authorities assigned quotas of settlers to each administrative unit and the task of collecting the required number of peasants was given to local peasant associations. Peasants were given minimal information about resettlement and then only the most positive. Settler candidates were recruited in relief camps, or as they arrived at feeding centres—at the worst point of the famine."

Another man who was actively involved in the resettlement programme in Wollo, but who wishes to remain anonymous, was also highly critical: "According to the government's policy guidelines, 150,000 households, half the total, were to be from Wollo region. Local authorities here were not certain how such a large number of people could be collected. Neither were they in a position to provide the necessary transport services and other logistical matters.

"In all the haste and confusion it was decided to assign quotas to each province. And thus officials of Ambassel province were given the task of preparing 12,000 households or 72,000 peasants for settlement. They in turn assigned quotas to each of the three districts of Ambassel province to collect the required number.

"In each *woreda* (sub-district) there were collection centres where peasants recruited for resettlement were temporarily housed until transport was available. From there, they were trucked to Haig, Serba and other small townships to await transportation to resettlement areas. In each of the primary and secondary staging points, peasants stayed for several days and nights in often appalling conditions, as a result of which some died. Worse still, thousands of peasants' families were separated; the number of children found abandoned at each of the transit points and at the project sites runs into thousands."

Problems in the new settlements

Ato Yimer Ali, an official in the Ambassel provincial office, Wollo, said that about 10% of the peasants sent to resettlement camps had returned to their communities by the middle of 1986: "A majority of the peasants concerned had abandoned their new 'homes' because of the hostility shown them by the local population in Metekel." A district peasant association official in the same province said some returnees had given hunger as the main reason. In some communities the returnees were treated as heroes and offered a variety of assistance and support.

The Ketto resettlement project was one of many established following the 1984-85 drought. It involved the movement of 42,811 drought victims from northern Wollo and Shoa regions to Wollega region, some 600 km southwest of Addis Ababa.

The main objective of the project was to provide the drought-affected population with the necessary infrastructural, social and agricultural services so that they could become self-sufficient. There was "a comprehensive package including the provision of urgent infrastructural services, and community development support to promote stability in the villages—including extension services in agriculture and tailoring crafts, and for women and development".

Social scientist Ato Meheret Ayenew made a preliminary investigation of the project: "Quite a lot of infrastructure has been invested in the Ketto resettlement complex. Much has been done to meet the basic social and economic needs of the resettlers. Several projects have been launched to enable the resettlement to become self-sufficient in the shortest possible time. But there are some indications that, four to five years after the population was brought here, they have not yet stabilised; few wish to consider Ketto their future home and permanent place of residence.

"By August 1989 the population had dropped from the original 42,811 to 35,626 and some 17% of the original resettler community have abandoned Ketto."

Indris Adem was brought to the settlement from Wollo without fully realising what was happening: "Back home, I used to be the breadwinner for my four beloved children and my wife. I was brought here some four years ago. At least I am not hungry here, but I feel more hunger for my family back home. I do not know whether my children and my wife are still alive. I would like to go back home. I would rather die in the place where I was born. As we say, 'Let the hyena of my home devour me.'"

Two other peasants from Wollo said that they found the climate unbearable, and although they are willing to stay in the settlement for some time, they and many of their fellow peasants are tired of eating nothing but sorghum and maize, the only crops they can raise in the area. One of them quoted a rhyme composed by local peasants: "Our sauce is maize, our drink is maize, our kids eat maize, we eat maize in the morning, we eat maize in the evening."

The settlers' complaints are understandable, for they came from a temperate climate where they used to grow a variety of crops, and find it difficult to adjust to the predominance of one or two.

Tadesse Haile, an agricultural extension service worker at the Ketto project, commented on the farming system. "Farming for settlers has been communal in Ketto since they arrived. The communal mode of land ownership and production is perhaps one of the factors which has undermined the enthusiasm of the new settlers and contributed to a significant desertion rate. They were all individual peasant farmers and had neither the commitment nor the experience of producers' cooperatives. Communal ownership of land and farming was imposed upon them by the government without their consent and participation."

In the communal farm the harvest is distributed to individual households on the basis of work points. Many settlers are bitter about what they consider to be an unfair system, as another piece of new folklore indicates: "There were 50 of us when we worked on the farm but we became 100 when we ate the harvest."

One of the most serious grievances of many settlers was that work on the land in Ketto was much harder than it had been at home. The settlers use hoes, for an average of 12-13 hours a day, tilling the soil, weeding and performing other activities on communal and private land. They cannot supplement their efforts by using oxen because these are vulnerable to the cattle disease in the area.

The people have serious health problems, too. Specialists have identified Ketto as a major area for water-borne diseases, and malaria, yellow fever, human and animal trypanosomiasis, and river blindness are endemic. Malaria has become so bad that some of the resettlement villages have decided to move and try again in new places.

Another cause of ill health with which the settlers were unfamiliar is the jigger flea, a type of sand fly found in lowland areas. Jiggers are a serious hazard in the dry season. The female burrows beneath the skin, entering mainly through the toes and hands. Unless the parasite is removed with a needle, it lays eggs and swelling develops, causing intense itching and inflammation. Wounds easily become infected. Controlling the fleas is difficult, as settlers do not have spare water with which to douse the floors of huts where the insects abound.

Settlers came to terms with the jiggers by personifying them, usually as female, in mocking rhyme. One village gave the jigger the name Akakkalac Denqu, Denqu meaning "Amazing One":

The one kindness of Akakkalac Denqu

Is that she does not distinguish

Between cadres and settlers.

Through the versatile and oft-recited rhymes, settlers expressed many of the frustrations of life in the settlements, their unhappiness at being in a strange country, and resentment at the status of party members. They often included a derogatory reference to the local Oromo population, whom settlers sometimes mocked for their jigger-damaged feet. The term *mojaleam* ("one with jiggers") has become a common form of insult among children.

Tension between settlers and local people

Inevitably, the large numbers of settlers encroached on the resources of the local people, and tension ensued. Ato Mekonnen Ibrie had been settled in Metekel. After his return to his home in Wollo, he related his experiences: "In one resettlement village in Metekel some 600 peasants from Wollo, including myself, had been settled within existing peasant associations. Local officials believed that the chosen peasant association had plenty of unused land to accommodate us all. However, the Bega [the local population] resented the decision because they claimed the land given to us newcomers was theirs. Apparently the officials failed to respond favourably to their complaint. Some Bega took direct action.

"In the months that followed several of the Wollo peasants were attacked and others killed. One of the victims was a relative of mine. I wished to take revenge on the Bega killers, but I couldn't. The security situation in the areas where we Wollo settlers lived deteriorated, with the Bega firing on non-Bega residents and travellers. Thank God, I have come back here and I am leading a very peaceful life with my fellow countrymen."

The Bega point of view was put by Balambaras Gog Mangua, a respected leader of one of the clans: "There are several kinds of natural resources within the boundary of each clan, all belonging to the collective. There are two categories of land which each clan member has a right to use for cultivation. First, there is land which is under cultivation, and second, land which is temporarily left fallow or unused. As the land in the first category becomes exhausted, new land from the second category is brought under cultivation. But the common practice of local officials in Metekel has been to consider the unutilised land in Bega communities as excess land for the benefit of new settlers.

"The clans usually also own forest or woodland which provides supplementary resources collectively. A clan also has access to large forest areas and water resources which are used for hunting or gathering. The Metekel resettlement was in just such an area utilised by the different Bega clans. So you see, there is little unused land around Bega communities. We Bega are threatened by the resettlement programme in Metekel. It will damage and eventually may even totally destroy the land-use system of our people. The appropriation of land for resettlement has denied us the use of the forest and other resources. And no serious attempts have been made to understand us and our system."

Another local said: "These settlers from Wollo cut down all the trees in the area. They ruined the land. All the forest is cut down because of them. The land in Wollo and Tigray is dry. We loved our land and looked after it, but they are clearing the forest and the rains have stopped."

Around Ketto, according to the local Oromo population, the presence of settlers has frightened away the wild animals and upset the ecological balance in the area. The settlers occupy a buffer zone between the local inhabitants and the predators. There is also a widespread feeling among both the local people and the settler community of being neglected by both development agencies and the government.

Dr Dessalegn Rahmato concludes: "The resettlement experience of the last decade or so may be viewed as an example of how to mismanage or lay the groundwork for the failure of settlement programmes. Everything that the settlement specialist, or even the average individual concerned with the success of settlement programmes, will work hard to avoid has been committed."

CHAPTER EIGHT

Full Circle

> War has destroyed everything. There are mines everywhere
> and people are scared to farm their land. It is war which [has
> forced us to leave our land]—someone does not leave their area
> just because of one or two years of drought!
> *Nebiat, an Eritrean now living in Sudan*

The final stage of the relationship between environmental
degradation and conflict is the way that war itself damages the
environment and so further contributes to the ecological problems
of a region, sowing the seeds for further strife. Thus the relationship
comes full circle. Eritrean academic **Zeremariam Fre** examines
the destruction taking place in Eritrea as a result of the war with
Ethiopia, and the legacy of environmental devastation which the
Eritrean people must now face.

The legacy of war
by Zeremariam Fre

The fundamental cause of the conflict is a political one: the
annexation of a country, a people and its resources. Ethiopia wants
Eritrea to remain part of Ethiopia because Ethiopia needs access to
the Red Sea. In this respect it can be said that the Eritrean-Ethiopian
conflict is also environmentally inspired, perhaps more so than is
often admitted. And while much has been written about the conflict
in general, little research has been done on the impact of the war on
the region's environment.

The war has bled the people of Eritrea and Ethiopia near to death;
and it is the biggest enemy of the Eritrean environment. After three

decades of bloody conflict, EPLF forces today have the upper hand. It is possible now to talk of a post-conflict scenario, but while Eritrea may well emerge politically as an independent state, it will be environmentally bankrupt.

Among the environment-related problems facing an emergent state will be acute land shortages in the densely populated plateau region; underdeveloped traditional farming techniques; a disused, cash-crop-oriented plantation sector; pastoralist underdevelopment and displacement; shortage of fodder, water and firewood; erratic rainfall; drought; periodic locust infestation; and refugee resettlement. These are semi-perennial problems which Eritrea shares with its neighbours and which will not simply go away once independence has been achieved.

Background: Eritrea

Eritrea was an Italian colony from 1890 until 1941, when it came under British administration. After the Second World War the Allies could not agree on the future of defeated Italy's ex-colony. Britain had encouraged nationalist aspirations in Eritrea, but Ethiopia pressed for the unification of Eritrea with Ethiopia. In 1952 the UN voted for the federation of Eritrea with Ethiopia, with limited powers of government vested in an elected Eritrean assembly. Ethiopia gradually undermined this assembly, and in 1962 pressed it to vote for its own abolition and the incorporation of Eritrea into Ethiopia.

Eritreans in exile and in underground movements at home were already demanding the complete separation of Eritrea from Ethiopia; the Eritrean Liberation Front (ELF) launched its first attacks on police and military targets in 1961. The Eritrean People's Liberation Front (EPLF), established in 1970, emerged as the dominant force in Eritrea after some years of internal struggle.

In Ethiopia, the regime of Emperor Haile Selassie fell in 1974. Power was seized by the armed forces, who ruled through a "co-ordinating committee": the Dergue. By 1977, Mengistu Haile Mariam had gained control of the Dergue.

The revolutionary government continued the Emperor's policy of opposition to Eritrean separatism. The Eritrean forces gained control of most of Eritrea by 1977, but the Ethiopian army retaliated, with Soviet help. War has continued ever since, and by 1990 the EPLF was in control of most of Eritrea, excluding the capital, Asmara.

Eritrea: the land and its resources

Eritrea has an estimated population of 4 million, 1 million of whom are refugees, made up of nine ethnic groups, of Hamitic, Cushitic and Nilotic origins, who speak nine different languages. It covers an area of 124,320 sq km, and its coast, 1,000 km in length, stretches from Ras Kasar in the north to Bab-el-mandab, at the southern tip of the Red Sea.

The physical environment consists of arid and semi-arid coastal plains, central plateau highlands, and northern massif and western lowlands or Sudan plains. The vegetation is as varied as the landscape, and this ecological and physical diversity means that a variety of crops, vegetables and fruits can be grown, and various livestock species reared.

The predominantly rural population depends on mixed farming, pastoralism, horticulture, wage labour, barter trade, cottage industries and, along the coast, limited fishing. Livestock production and crop cultivation are by far the most important economic occupations in rural Eritrea.

Land distribution in the country falls into two major categories. The first includes *diesa* (communal land), which belongs to village communities composed of extended families, and *resti* (inherited land), which is privately owned. This type of land tenure is found mainly in the plateau or Kebesa region, as well as in other highland areas where traditional crop farming is extensive.

The other major category is the *dominale* (state land), which embraces the most spacious and fertile lowland regions in the west, east, northeast, and parts of the plateau. During the Italian occupation, such areas were developed for concession agriculture, which concentrated on plantation crops such as cotton, sesame and citrus. This type of development gave rise to the displacement of pastoralists, from areas which they claim were traditional dry-season grazing lands, and attracted an influx of peasant groups from more populated areas. This has led to some friction between groups over resources.

Given the erratic nature of seasonal rainfall in Eritrea, irrigated rather than rainfed agriculture seems to have the greatest potential for increasing food production. During the peaceful years from 1952 to 1960, a total of 400,000 hectares of land depended on irrigation [1]. Eritrea was then a leading exporter of fresh fruits, from the Horn to the Middle East. The country was also a major exporter of live animals and animal by-products, primarily to the Middle East, with much of the livestock originating in pastoralist areas. The cross- border livestock trade with east Sudan continues, on a much reduced but still considerable scale.

During the Italian colonial period, 1885-1941, Eritrea became an increasingly industrialised and urban state. After the Second World War there was a considerable industrial boom, based on local raw materials. Textiles, food products, glassware, beer, fibre and paper, soap, oil seed and tobacco products were manufactured for the domestic and international markets. By 1950 there were more than 100,000 industrial workers with a strong trade union movement. With its long coastline, Eritrea has a promising marine industry. Processing of fish and other marine products thrived in peacetime.

The mineral and marine resources remain under-exploited. Mineral finds include gold, copper, silver, iron ore, kaolin, mica, marble, petroleum, asbestos, manganese, titanium and nickel.

In a country which is torn apart by war, famine and ecological crisis, much of the above information now seems like history. The post-war scenario looks completely different, its main features being a devastated environment and the displacement of half of the civilian population.

Environmental degradation

This is not to say that degradation, due to overgrazing and high population densities of both people and livestock in the highland regions of Eritrea, was not already well advanced before the war. Firewood and construction materials were already in short supply, although not as desperately as today. Then, the survival strategy of Eritrean peasants was to migrate to grazing and agricultural land in less populated areas, around the green belt known as *bahri* and to the western lowlands, particularly the Gash and Setit areas. Eritrea has also experienced serious locust infestation, as have other countries in the region. Swarms of these pests have devastated vast areas three or four times in the last 30 years.

But the war is now the single most important factor of degradation in Eritrea. The clearing of forest reserves by troops, intense bombing raids of civilian targets, the scattering of land mines over wide areas and the concentration of people in and around security hamlets—all are rapidly accelerating the deterioration of an already fragile ecology and rural economy. And the constant use

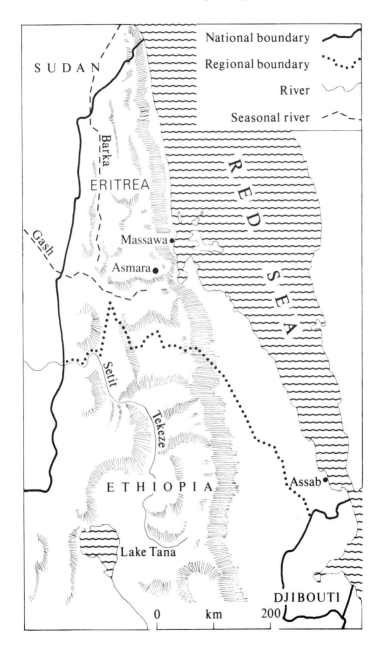

National boundary

Regional boundary

River

Seasonal river

SUDAN

Barka

ERITREA

Gash

Massawa

Asmara

RED SEA

Setit

Tekeze

ETHIOPIA

Assab

Lake Tana

DJIBOUTI

0   km   200

of heavy weapons, including MiG aircraft carrying napalm and defoliants; a policy of bush clearance of areas believed to be guerilla hideouts; and the Ethiopian troops' demand for fuelwood have all greatly reduced plant cover.

It is difficult at this stage to quantify the overall environmental impact of the war but there are many eye-witness accounts of areas where forests have been destroyed, the flora and fauna have been devastated and the livestock population drastically reduced, as well as of overfishing of the Red Sea by Soviet vessels using mines.

Degradation caused by war

The one ubiquitous touch of green is the thorny acacia, whose spreading branches can hide anything from a nomad family to a tank, from sacks of wheat flour to a literacy class.
Joseph Marand (foreign journalist visiting Eritrea, 1987)

[The Eritrean guerillas] found natural fortresses in the semi- arid lowlands, where nomadism is the main form of life, and in the extremely hilly areas that complicate the movements of a regular [Ethiopian] army.
B.W. Semait (Ethiopian writer, 1989)

For the Ethiopian trooper a green valley surrounded by bare mountains is a guerilla haven which should be cleared for better security. The Eritrean fighter considers trees and green valleys his refuge, his camouflage and his base. Thus the protection of the forest cover and vegetation on such valleys is essential to his survival.

In fact, after three decades of war, much of the Eritrean forest has been cleared. The Ethiopian army in Eritrea, estimated to be 150,000 strong, is concentrated in and around major towns, from where it threatens the surrounding forest and water resources. Such an army requires not only thousands of tonnes of firewood each year, but also a large supply of construction materials to build shelters and trenches. Villagers around Asmara, the capital city, report that Ethiopian soldiers are so desperate for firewood that they have snatched wooden farm implements from farmers and uprooted the main wooden frames of the *hdmo* (traditional hamlets) for fuel.

The eastern flank of Asmara was for decades covered by a thick eucalyptus forest, some 200 hectares in area, called Bet-Giorghis, which means home of St George. The plantation was established by the Italians during 1930 and survived well until 1975. The Ethiopian

Neil Cooper/Panos Pictures

"The Eritrean fighter considers trees and green valleys his refuge, his camouflage and his base."

army in and around Asmara is estimated to be between 60,000 and 75,000 strong. According to the Forestry Department of the Ethiopian Ministry of Agriculture in Asmara, the army did not have any serious effect on the forest until it started to cut it down in 1976. The motive was partly "security", to open up the forest against what were called possible "rebel incursions" into Asmara. They also desperately wanted firewood. The Forestry Department was not consulted as to which trees should and should not be felled.

Once the forest was opened up, the civilian population became involved, cutting trees to meet its own continuing firewood needs. Gradually, the Eritrean capital was denuded of its only major forest. Small village-run forest reserves around Asmara were also cleared. According to sources in the Forestry Department, the army is currently in the process of clearing the green belt itself in Mrara and Solomona districts in the east. These are very important coffee-growing areas with high agricultural and pastoral potential, but the peasants have now been barred from using them. The green belt is also an important source of firewood for the civilian population in and around Asmara. Much of the area has now been covered with land mines, planted by the army against EPLF forces, making access dangerous.

A different approach

The EPLF for its part not only depends greatly on forest resources, but also sees the maintenance of available vegetation as vital to its own survival. There is little evidence to suggest that the EPLF deliberately clears forests. Unlike the Ethiopian army, which is concentrated primarily around urban centres, the Eritrean army is widely spread out. By using mud and stone instead of wood for building, it has reduced its need for wood.

The army still lacks firewood and grazing resources—increasingly so as the conflict drags on. A recent study, based on satellite data and fieldwork by two researchers from the Open University in Britain, showed that the rate of environmental degradation is much higher in areas under the control of the Ethiopian government than those held by the EPLF, and that forest cover has actually increased in EPLF base areas [2].

In the contested zones, where the Ethiopian army has little or no access, MiG fighters are used to bomb "enemy territory". There are eye-witness accounts of the extensive use of napalm by Ethiopian MiG fighters in northern Eritrea. The civilian population in that region speak of "fire raining from the skies eating everything in its way; even the tortoise in its hard shell cannot survive such fire".

One young victim was a 12-year-old shepherdess called Halima Osman: "I was herding my flock of sheep and goats on the hilltop overlooking Zara valley where our village was situated. One morning, two planes kept hovering over us. I tried to hide under a tree but some of my goats and sheep were white-coated and they attracted the pilots' attention. After one hour the planes returned again and poured fire on us. Most of my sheep and goats were burnt alive. As you can see, all my body is burnt."

After six months' treatment, Halima recovered but only partially. Abandoned hamlets, disfigured trees, poisoned wells and dying fauna also show the clear impact of bombing. But as Halima's story shows, the disruption to people's lives is extreme, often destroying their ability to work in the environment again, or to contribute to its rehabilitation.

The war has displaced an estimated half a million people within Eritrea and has led to higher population concentrations in the Gash and Setit areas, where communities representing seven out of the nine ethnic groups are to be found, competing for agricultural land, water and grazing resources (see Chapter Three, p51). The potential for inter-ethnic conflict in this area is considerable, but the cessation of hostilities between Ethiopia and Eritrea could reduce some of the competition. After independence, many of the settlers are likely to return to their traditional home base. But others come from areas too degraded to support any form of livelihood, so tensions are likely to continue.

Furthermore, since the Ethiopian government lost control of most of rural Eritrea, over two decades ago, farmers have been denied basic agricultural inputs, and there have been no government-sponsored attempts at environmental rehabilitation or conservation. The area which is outside government control, about 80-90% of the countryside, is considered enemy territory. EPLF attempts at large-scale environmental rehabilitation programmes have been hampered by the changing war situation, and are limited to areas which they firmly control.

Security hamlets

Once the Ethiopian government realised that it was losing control over the countryside, starting in the late 1960s, they introduced the idea of "security hamlets". What began as a small project in western Eritrea is now national policy. It involves the large-scale rounding up of traditionally scattered villages to areas designated by the government. Most of the villages were burned down by the army on the basis that they suspected the villagers were guerilla collaborators. These very villagers were then told that they would be safer in the security hamlets, which they themselves would have to build and which are under the army's charge.

There are a number of environmentally negative implications of these hamlets. First, usual working hours among peasant groups in peace time are between 5 am and 8 pm, depending on seasonal labour demands. In the government-controlled security hamlets there is a dawn to dusk curfew (6 am to 6 pm), which drastically reduces free movement and working hours. The absence of night grazing (a crucial part of good cattle management), and of an early start to farming activities such as weeding and oxen ploughing have severely curtailed food production in these areas. And if cattle go astray at night, peasants cannot venture outside to fetch them. Many peasants cannot return to their traditional grazing and farm lands either, because such areas are outside the security hamlet zone, which covers a 10 km radius.

The second environmental impact of the security hamlets, the populations of which range from 500 to 6,000 households, is that they contain huge concentrations of livestock and people. No advance preparation is made to accommodate such densities, so there is intense competition over grazing and farm land, firewood and water, making the surrounding locations the most degraded in the country. The army around the security hamlets also requires water and shelter. The civilians in the hamlets are so desperate for firewood that they burn dried dung and straw, valuable sources of fertiliser and animal fodder.

Living in and around concentrated security hamlets, as opposed to the more scattered traditional pattern of settlement, effectively diminishes the ability of rural society to be economically self-sufficient. Farmers can no longer protect or maintain the terraces on their now-abandoned settlements. Pastoralists have lost their access to grazing lands. Residents of security hamlets require travel permits to go to the nearest village or town. They cannot mix freely and voluntarily with other groups through trade, wage labour, social and cultural activities and so on. The peripheral areas around the security hamlets are dotted with anti-personnel mines, supposedly to stop Eritrean guerilla incursion to such villages. Yet civilians and livestock often get blown up by the mines, and other peasants are deterred from visiting the villages for fear of these devices.

Pastoralists

The loss of grazing land, the fear and insecurity caused by the state of emergency, and the high livestock taxation imposed by the government, have all pushed many pastoralists to divert their livestock trade to eastern Sudan. An Eritrean peasant laments: "The Sudanese have got our people and cattle on the cheap," referring to Eritrean refugees being cheap labour and Eritrean cattle providing cheap meat for the Sudanese.

Andu Kifle is an agro-pastoralist farmer from the small village of Adi-Werhi in Eritrea's Hamasien plateau. Andu and his two adult sons, Mehari and Keleta, used to take advantage of the winter rains (November-February) by moving with their livestock to the *bahri* (green belt), 140 km east of Adi-Werhi where the rest of the family remained. Farming on the mainly state- owned *dominale* land in the green belt, Andu and his sons would get a reasonable harvest in February and March and return to Adi-Werhi by April, bringing sacks of grain, butter, ghee and salt as rewards for their labour. A great deal of bartering between farmers and pastoralists takes place in these areas. Grain is exchanged for dairy products and salt, and hired pastoralist labour is remunerated in cash or kind.

At the onset of the May rains, one son would return to the green belt to collect the pair of draught oxen left there with relatives. From May until October the whole family was busy cultivating in their plateau village. After the harvest and a few months' rest, the farming cycle started again.

This was the case until 1985, when Andu Kifle and his family, along with several hundred villagers from surrounding areas, were transferred to a new security hamlet called Inwet, where their movement is restricted to a 10 km radius. Their whole agricultural system and pattern of life broke down. Andu sums up the feelings of many peasants: "We are like voiceless prisoners in these security hamlets. We have some oxen but not the land to plough, we have the cattle but we cannot graze freely. What choice do we have other than to starve? Yet we have harmed no one."

Mohamed Nawd is a cattle owner from the village of Ad-Ghedem in the southwestern Barka, in the western lowlands. Traditionally, the cattle migrate to the wet-season and dry-season camps within tribal territory, over a radius of 40-100 km. During the long dry season (December-April), the non-milking cattle are taken 500 km south to graze deep in the Gonder area of northern Ethiopia and southeast Sudan. Only able-bodied men migrate with the cattle for these long distances, while families remain in the traditional home territory.

Since 1978, the wet-season camps and territory have come under the control of the EPLF and the dry-season camp has until recently been under the control of Ethiopian troops. The Nawd family were unable to continue with pastoralist activities and fled the constant air strikes by Ethiopian MiGs, leaving their cattle behind. They have been in refugee camps on the Sudan border since 1984.

Another refugee in Sudan is Mohamed Arey, a pastoralist from northern Eritrea. In 1982 his 150 cattle were looted by the Ethiopian army while grazing in a valley near his village: "They beat me up and asked me to slaughter two of the cows for them. I did so and then ran away, taking their horns with me. I am now a refugee in Sudan. In front of my hut I have the horns pegged upright. I water them every morning, hoping that my cows will one day grow."

Plans for the future

Once peace has been achieved the EPLF is expected to draw up an environmental action plan with strong community participation. The EPLF's current agricultural policy is geared towards self-sufficiency. The main objectives are to improve peasant production and to remain as independent as possible of imported agricultural inputs and foodstuffs. In the short term, this involves resettling thousands of Eritreans displaced from zones of drought and war. In the long term, the EPLF aims to resettle the hundreds of thousands of Eritrean peasants now living as refugees in neighbouring countries and to decrease dependence on outside aid in times of drought and war-induced shortages.

Assuming that there is peace after the present conflict is over, there is scope for regional cooperation between the war-torn countries of the region. There have always been trading, cultural, socio-economic and historical ties among the peoples of the Horn. The hope is that such links will one day be revived and that the environmental crisis can be tackled as a regional problem.

CHAPTER NINE

Responses

> Now there was a famine in the land....So Isaac went to the valley
> of Gerar and dwelt there....But when Isaac's servants dug in the
> valley and found a well of springing water, the herdsmen of Gerar
> quarrelled with Isaac's herdsmen, saying "The water is ours". So
> he called the well Esek, Contention, because they contended with
> him. Then they dug another well, and they quarrelled over that also;
> so he called it Sitnah, Enmity.
> (The Book of Genesis 26:1,17-21)

The Book of Genesis is a reminder that the Greenwar tale is not a
new one. The Qur'an offers an equally powerful picture of concern
over natural resources. One verse can even be interpreted as
encouraging the people to overthrow rulers who ignore
environmental degradation: "Obey not the command of the wasteful
who spread corruption on the earth." (The Poets XXVI:151-2).

As *Greenwar* shows, competition and cooperation over use of
resources have always been part of life in the Sahel. What is
changing is the increasing level of violence and desperation— and
the scale of conflict. There is a complex web of causes behind the
growth of instability and bloodshed, but the deterioration of the
natural resource base is increasingly a key factor. This phenomenon
is not peculiar to the Sahel, but the region is in the frontline of
environmental bankruptcy and associated conflict.

Interdependence

Interdependence and co-existence were once the dominant features
of the Sahelian people's relationship with each other and with their
environment.

Chad's Lake Fitri is the site of a Garden of Eden-type legend, where pastoralists and farmers once co-existed peacefully. The sultan would ask his farmers to prepare corridors for the herders' animals to pass along, on their way to the lakeside grass. In return, the herders respected the customary authorities and traditions of the lakeside farmers. In Senegal, too, the herders "lived in symbiosis" with nature "without any clashes or deterioration, for centuries".

In Burkina Faso the head of a women's group tells how "in our grandparents' time there was an abundance here, and people from different villages tried to outdo each other in kindness. Today it is different, because there isn't enough rain, the harvests are bad and the men are less kind".

Obviously, the picture was not one of undisturbed peace and harmony, as some of the elderly people interviewed for *Greenwar* reminded the authors. Around Lake Fitri "it was impossible to control the cows completely when they went through those lush fields; sometimes an animal would break away from the herd and pull out some leaves or stems", which provided an ideal excuse for farmers to demand compensation. But it is equally clear that across the Sahel the situation has deteriorated. What were once isolated incidents of hostility have become commonplace.

Bouki the hyena, the resourceful character in many Wolof stories in Senegal, says: "The greediest one of all is the poor man." How come? "Ask him for something; he is bound to say no." When the Sahelian poor are forced "to say no", it is the first indication that social and political mechanisms are failing, and that insecurity is eroding traditional means of containing and defusing competition over resources. And as the region sinks deeper into environmental bankruptcy, the poor are increasingly forced "to say no".

The complex web

The various chapters in this book have identified and analysed many reasons for the rising level of tension in the Sahel. One of the most widespread is that changing patterns of land use have put heavy pressures on herders and small farmers, as the son of Sheikh El Zein of the Lahawin pastoralists in east Sudan explains: "When the land started to shrink before our eyes, those of us who used to live in harmony started to grumble at each other...". Throughout the Sahel centuries-old routes between traditional pastures have been disrupted: "When animals need to move...they find in their path large areas of land stripped of trees and wild grasses. They cannot take a step without walking into a field."

The balance between people and their environment is being upset, threatening their ability to meet their most basic needs. As competition grows for dwindling resources, tension often flares into open hostility.

In the Sahel, government action more often exacerbates than relieves the situation. *Greenwar* contains examples of state intervention in favour of one particular ethnic group in west Sudan, of one economic sector in Mauritania, and in favour of large-scale, mechanised farming in east Sudan. "Our land is lost to the owners of farms," laments Sheikh El Zein.

Legislation usually reinforces these destructive processes. Land has been distributed for tractor cultivation by wealthy farmers in Sudan on the assumption that unregistered land is empty, so that the pastoralists' grazing lands are taken away from them by a central administration which seems to ignore or deliberately undermine their interests. The landholding code in newly independent Senegal instituted western-style tenure, reflecting the fact that "the law-makers of the young state had one concern: to lay the basis for an increase in agricultural production".

All too often, the law is used to defend the wealthy. Pastoralists in particular—"men without land"—often lose out in land disputes: their way of life does not easily fit in with the demands of the modern state. Women, too, frequently find land-tenure codes and traditions weighted against them. They are often the last to be given access to a plot in the family landholdings and what land they do have is rarely of good quality. Again, this is not new. One Mauritanian proverb goes: "Land is a father who does not recognise his daughters." But as social disruption spreads across the Sahel, leaving increasing numbers of women as heads of households, their need for land to grow food becomes ever more acute.

Those administering the law are rarely impartial. Niger Minister Khamed Abdoulaye, a member of the Tuareg pastoralist people, admits that "the gendarmes...mostly behave as if they were on conquered territory, and because of this they symbolise pure violence in the eyes of the [pastoralist] population".

The instability sparked off by environmental pressures inevitably breeds further insecurity. Fearful of robbery and violence, people arm themselves to protect their land, animals, and

Neil Cooper/Panos Pictures

The recycling of military hardware, as in this market, is an increasingly common sight in the Sahel.

families. In virtually all of the villages Cheik Kolla Maïga visited in northern Burkina Faso, there are men carrying guns, which they say are necessary to protect their possessions. "How do you get them?" he asked. "In Mali, in exchange for a camel, you can get a good gun," was the reply.

Once conflict has broken out, the ready availability of weapons can make any violence more deadly, and move the Greenwar cycle on to another level of intensity. Osman Aboker Adam, a chief from west Sudan, is now in a camp for the displaced. "It is difficult to resolve the conflict now", he says, "because each group has bought weapons to fight with. These armed tribes have become robbers, looters and highwaymen, who use the gun to stay alive."

Sudanese police captain Hassan Kashaba, from Kassala province near the border with Ethiopia, reports "repeated incidents" of intertribal rivalry, with "modern automatic guns and fast Land Cruisers".

Today, many thousands of *faloul* (rural bandits) roam throughout this lawless and unstable border area. Many are young men—and not a few are children, caught up in situations where family or community solidarity has been strained to breaking point. Sergeant Osman, the police chief in Wad el Hileau, knows of "about 150 refugee children" now engaged in crime in this one village. He fears that they are growing up to be urban *faloul*. Nafissa Abdel Rahim reports on the large proportion of vagrant children in Khartoum who are from displaced families.

Poverty and powerlessness often breed prejudice. In the dispute between Senegal and Mauritania, "the most disadvantaged tended to blame all their ills on the 'others', the 'foreigners'. Xenophobia was rampant". But such reactions are not restricted to the poorest sections of society, although they are usually those first hit by the conflict which may result.

The disruption caused by environmental decline is immense. Whole communities are forced to give up their traditional livelihoods because of drought, or because of eroded and exhausted land. "They had to flee to towns to become labourers," says farmer Mohamed Idris from west Sudan, of his fellow Fur farmers.

As well as creating new tensions, the Greenwar factor feeds into existing political and racial antagonisms. Sometimes the result is that whole communities become refugees to escape direct combat. "I can truly say I lost all my property in this conflict," says Osman Abaker Adam from west Sudan. "My brother was killed by the Arabs and my first wife died on our way   [to a camp for the displaced]. There are many other farmers ...who fled the war zones."

The dispossessed move to shanty towns or new settlements, where their presence usually causes yet more tension and conflict, and puts further demands on an already overstretched environment near the urban centres. Nafissa Abdel Rahim interviewed men and women in camps around Khartoum who are no longer able to feed their families, and who must live with the humiliation of being unable to fulfil traditional cultural obligations, such as making a *karama* (sacrifice) for a newborn child.

In Ethiopia, the state attempted to solve its increasing political and ecological crises through deliberate resettlement. This "solution" creates yet more problems. "Misery and suffering characterised the entire resettlement operation," says an Ethiopian academic who has studied the programme. Fallow land in the resettlement area was considered as "unused" and was reallocated to settlers by ignorant officials, fuelling further grievances. Yet again, according to Balambaras Gog Mangua, clan leader in a Bega village where people were resettled, "no serious attempts have been made to understand us or our system".

Environmental degradation may fuel conflict but the reverse is also true. For decades, the Eritreans have fought the government of Ethiopia. "War has destroyed everything," says a refugee in Sudan. Eritrean academic Zeremariam Fre argues that "the war has bled the people of Eritrea and Ethiopia near to death; and it is the biggest enemy of the Eritrean environment". Whatever the political or military outcome, the Eritrean people will inherit an environmentally bankrupt land. And so the vicious cycle of environmental decline, tense competition for dwindling resources, increasing hostility, intercommunal fighting, social and political breakdown, civil and interstate war turns full circle.

Can this cycle be broken?

The state's answer

Sahelian governments, like many elsewhere, usually pay attention to the political crises in the region, but fail to address the substantive issue of natural resource depletion. One of their "answers" has been to increase their military strength. Between 1966 and 1989, a period of little more than 20 years, the armed forces personnel of the nine Sahelian countries considered in *Greenwar* increased more than sixfold, from 79,000 to 515,000 [1].

In parallel to the increases in armed forces personnel, there has been a substantial growth in armaments. Accurate figures are hard to obtain, since both suppliers and recipients are reluctant to release details. But the only factors which act as an effective brake on arms imports seem to be lack of economic resources or of arms donors.

The growth in arms supplied to the Sahel is not just in quantity, but also in the type of weapons. Many of the local conflicts described in this study have been carried out with minimal military equipment. But in recent years, Sahelian governments have been provided with sophisticated weapons systems including advanced jet fighter aircraft and a wide range of tanks, armoured personnel carriers and long-range heavy artillery. Many modern guns are light and simple to operate. One consequence is that children can now play a role in warfare which was unimaginable 20 years ago. In many instances, Sahelian children are no longer just the primary victims of the region's conflicts—they are active protagonists. Many children, like those on the border between Sudan and Ethiopia, know no other life.

These weapons may have originally been intended to protect citizens from attack, but they have inevitably raised the stakes in confrontations over environmental issues. One consequence is a tendency to use military force in response to non-military challenges. The reaction of Sahelian governments to political tensions associated with environmental resource issues seems increasingly to be a military one—as the stories of the Tuareg protest and the conflict over the Beli River demonstrate.

Greenwar shows us that in a semi-subsistence economy, the easiest form of attack is to destroy the natural resource base of your opponent. The grim reality is that the means of survival for ordinary citizens—their resources—have become logical targets for the state in Sahelian warfare [2]. There are examples, as with the four-nation commission working to sort out potential boundary conflicts over Lake Chad, of positive government action to avert hostilities. But short-term attempts to suppress conflict rather than to analyse and tackle its underlying causes have been far more common.

The response of the outside world

Such indictments should not be directed at Sahelian governments alone, for they do not operate in a vacuum.

The international community must bear its share of

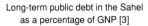

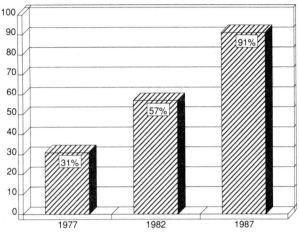

Long-term public debt in the Sahel
as a percentage of GNP [3]

responsibility. Unequal terms of world trade and falling commodity prices all impose enormous constraints on Sahelian commerce and production, forcing inappropriate agricultural development and overexploitation of land.

The debt crisis has nevertheless been a further powerful demonstration of Sahelian governments' commitment to the military option. The Sahel's debt may not appear significant when compared to other regions of the South, but it is strangling the region. Yet the cuts in government spending which it forces do not appear to be having any impact on military expenditure, only on "soft" longer-term investments. Unless this pattern can be reversed, the Sahel is likely to experience further environmental degradation and further escalations in conflict .

What can aid achieve?

In this context of disadvantageous patterns of world trade and of distorted government priorities, it is unlikely that international aid can have any profound or longlasting effect. This is worth stressing, because official development assistance to the Sahel has been higher than to any other region of the Third World, and has continued to rise. By 1988 it had reached US$55 per head [4], as compared to US$14.6 in Bangladesh, US$22.2 in Nepal and US$2.6 in India [5].

Following the droughts of the 1970s and 1980s, aid organisations did show increased concern with environmental degradation. After the 1974-75 drought, donors and Sahelian governments agreed to give priority to the key rural development sector, which includes assistance to crop production, to pastoralism and to environmental protection measures. Taking the countries grouped together in CILSS as a whole (Senegal, Mauritania, Mali, Niger, Burkina Faso and Chad), aid to this sector doubled between 1975 and 1980. But between 1980 and 1987, the position was reversed, and external aid to rural development became a decreasing component of aid.

Pastoralism remained the poor relation throughout this time. In the period 1980-87, support to Sahelian pastoralism (again in the CILSS countries) represented around 2% of total aid, with financial volumes actually decreasing. Similarly, support to the "ecology and forests" sector fell to around 1% of total commitments by 1987.

The way forward?

There is no single solution to the Sahel's slide into environmental bankruptcy and bloodshed, just as there is no single cause. But the first element of any solution must be an understanding of the Greenwar phenomenon and the way that it links violence to the environment with violence to humankind.

Central to that understanding is the need for regional cooperation. The wind, the rain and the rivers do not recognise frontiers laid down when Britain, France and Italy carved up the region in colonial times. States which deal in isolation with the problem of declining natural resources are bound to come into conflict with other governments. The very soil on which one Sahelian country depends may have come from a neighbouring state. The Gezira, a triangular fertile plain between the White and Blue Niles which has provided key foreign exchange for Sudan over the years, is formed by sediment carried down mainly by the Blue Nile from the Ethiopian highlands.

The need to see beyond communal, regional or national needs runs right through resource conservation and allocation. The impossibility of establishing exclusive rights over the earth's resources was illustrated by the Habarje'lo elders, in the Somali tribal war of the 1950s, who claimed that they had some rights in the disputed area of grazing land since the clouds which nourished the grass there had been formed in the Habarje'lo's own northern highlands.

Greenwars are likely to increase. Water has been a major source of conflict in the region—and there is a risk that it will become more so as a result of global warming. Some computer models predict a severe decline in the region's rainfall over the coming decades. Increasing demands for irrigated agriculture and for industrial consumption are also likely to play their part in throwing water supply and demand perilously off balance.

Priorities

The Panos Institute has not attempted to draw up a precise set of recommendations from the broad range of materials and perceptions which make up *Greenwar*. This does not pretend to be a prescriptive book, but it does throw certain factors into strong relief.

One is that governments and international agencies alike have been slow to learn from their failures, and that the exchange and the dissemination of information across the region need far more attention. The fruits of research and planning are too rarely communicated in any useful way to people working in the field, while the idea that peasant farmers and pastoralists possess valuable insights into their own environment is hardly ever acknowledged by Sahelian policymakers.

Although *Greenwar* is a study of the Sahelian region, its lesson that peacekeeping and environmental recovery are intimately connected is relevant to many parts of the world. In nearby Turkey, the government has effectively decided on the amount of water its downstream neighbours Syria and Iraq will receive, by unilaterally constructing a major set of dams on the Euphrates. Similarly, Jordan faces the worst water crisis in the Middle East, claiming that Syria and Israel are systematically stealing its share of the Yarmuk River water.

The World Bank has now begun circulating discussion papers which argue that past concepts of national sovereignty are no longer sufficient for a world characterised by ever-increasing ecological interdependence among nations [6]. The United Nations Environment Programme (UNEP) publishes an impressive list of 140 international treaties and agreements on the environment. But as yet there have been few concrete examples of this theoretical change having any impact on the way governments, North and South, are dealing with the Greenwar factor.

While it may not be possible to change the natural characteristics of the land and climate of the Sahel, nor feasible to reduce the immediate pressure of increasing population, land can be used in ways that better protect its productivity, and resources can be allocated so that conflict is less likely. Giving a voice to the poor is an integral part of this process. For as the poor become increasingly dispossessed, forced to cultivate ever more marginal areas, the conditions which fuel ecological degradation spread over more of the earth's fragile drylands.

All over the world, a lack of people's participation in setting priorities and implementing them has undermined the achievement of sustainable development.

One key to breaking the vicious downward spiral of accelerating environmental decline and increasing conflict will surely be found in establishing greater local control over resource allocation. This requires a long-term commitment to the processes of democratisation which are currently being debated and fought for in many Sahelian countries.

The aim of that process is to ensure that all sections of the community, particularly those whose voices have been ignored for so long, have more control over the resources which they need to survive. It is a fight to get the priorities of the powerless on to the agenda of the state and its decisionmaking mechanisms. Rural voices must not be drowned out by urban voices, pastoralists' voices must be heard as well as farmers' voices, and women's voices of all sectors of society must be allowed to carry loud and clear.

That vision is one which has relevance far beyond the Sahel.

Nigel Twose
The Panos Institute

Acknowledgements

This book is the result of many people's work, ideas and comments. Towards the end of 1989, the Panos Institute contacted Sahelian non-governmental organisations, academics and journalists to discuss the idea of *Greenwar*. Once authors from each of the region's countries had agreed to participate, Panos organised a workshop in 1990 in Ouagadougou, Burkina Faso. When themes and approaches had been decided upon, each author contributed a manuscript on a topic which seemed most important in her or his own country. Nafissa Abdel Rahim, one of the Sudanese participants, then spent time in the Panos-London offices working with the editorial department on the book.

Others whose help was invaluable at this stage include Jennie Street, Heywote Bekele and Kitty Warnock. The text has also benefited from the comments of readers, including Jon Tinker, Dr Nigel Cross, Dr Camilla Toulmin and Dr Abebe Zegeye, and staff of Oxfam and the International Peace Research Institute (PRIO) in Oslo. Thanks are also due to the many Sahelian communities and individuals who received the authors so warmly during the fieldwork.

Notes

Introduction   What is Greenwar?

1. See, among others, Hjort af Ornäs, Anders and Salih, M. A. Mohamed (eds), *Ecology and Politics, Environmental Stress and Security in Africa*, Scandinavian Institute of African Studies, Uppsala, Sweden, 1989; *Environmental Security: A Report Contributing to the Concept of Comprehensive International Security*, PRIO/UNEP, Oslo/Nairobi, 1989; and Westing, Arthur, "Ecology, International Understanding, and Peace", UNEP, paper for the International Conference on Environmental Cooperation, Telemark, Norway, June 1988.

Chapter One   The Sahel

1. Davidson, Basil, *Africa in History*, Paladin Books, Herts, England, 1974.
2. Calculated from *Environmental Data Report*, UNEP, 1989/90, second edition, Blackwell, Oxford.
3. Cross, Nigel, *The Sahel: The Peoples' Right to Development*, Minority Rights Group, London, 1990.
4. *World Resources 1988-89*, Report by the World Resources Institute and the Institute for Environment and Development, with UNDP, Oxford University Press.
5. See, among others, de Vries, Penning, *La Productivité des Pâturages Saheliens*, Wageningen, 1982.

Chapter Two   Traditional Competition

1. Samatar, A., "The State, Agrarian Change and Crisis of Hegemony in Somalia", 1988.
2. Lewis, I. M., *A Pastoral Democracy*, published for African International Institute, Oxford University Press, 1982.

Chapter Three   Ancient Rivalry

1. *Environmental Data Report*, UNEP, 1989/90, op. cit.
2 Information from The Animal Resources Sub-commission, Agriculture Commission, Eritrea 1984.

Chapter Four   The Role of the State

1. *L'Express*, Paris, 22 June 1990.
2. Interview in *Le Sahel*, Niamey, 18 June 1990.
3. Procès-verbal de la rencontre entre la délégation du gouvernement du Mali et la délégation du mouvement populaire de l'Azaouad et du Front Islamique Arabe de l'Azaouad à Tamanrasset les 5 et 6 janvier 1991.

Chapter Five   Three Rivers

1. Grainger, Alan, *Desertification*, Earthscan, London, 1982.
2. International Court of Justice Communiqué, The Hague, No. 86/18.
3. *Sudanow*, Khartoum, July 1990.
4. "Egypt finds water beneath its sea of sand", Pugh, Deborah, Panos Features, London, 19 July 1990.
5. Dr Tvedt Terje, in a lecture given at the International Peace Research Institute (PRIO), Oslo, 11 June 1990.
6. Khamisa Baya, Beatrice, "Aid at a standstill", *War Wounds*, Panos Publications, London, 1988, p22.

Chapter Seven   Displacement

1. In December 1990 this spontaneous settlement was moved by the authorities to Jebel Awlia.
2. Survey by The Sudan Council of Churches, 1989.
3. Ethiopia's population growth in 1990 had declined to 2% per annum, which gives a doubling time of 34 years.
4. Rahmato, Dessalegn, "Rural resettlement in post-revolutionary Ethiopia—problems and prospects", paper prepared for the National Conference on Population Issues in Ethiopia's National Development, Institute of Development Research, University of Addis Ababa, July 1989.
5. Ibid.
6. *Ethiopia: more light on resettlement*, Survival International, London, 1991.

Chapter Eight   Full Circle

1. UN Commission, 1951.
2. Berhe, S.M. et al., "Water Resources for Rural Development in Eritrea", Department of Earth Sciences, Open University, Milton Keynes, England, 1989.

Chapter Nine   Responses

1. *The Military Balance*, International Institute for Strategic Studies, London. Figures refer to Burkina Faso, Chad, Ethiopia, Mali, Mauritania, Niger, Senegal, Somalia and Sudan. These figures do not include paramilitary units, which in some cases are larger and better equipped than the regular forces. Nor do they include armed personnel attached to forestry services.
2. For a deeper analysis of state responses see Duffield, Mark, "War and Famine in Africa", internal report, Oxfam, 1990.
3. Calculated from the *World Development Report 1990*, World Bank, Oxford University Press. Refers to Burkina Faso, Chad, Ethiopia, Mali, Mauritania, Niger, Senegal, Somalia and Sudan. These averages across nine countries must be treated with some caution, but they are consistent with the growth of the problem in individual countries.
4. Calculated from ibid. The same note of caution applies.
5. Calculated from ibid.
6. See, for example, Colby, Michael E., "Environmental management in development: the evolution of paradigms", World Bank discussion paper, No 80.